DRUG EDUCATION LIBRARY

STEROIDS AND OTHER
PERFORMANCE-ENHANCING
DRUGS

Jordan Rizzieri

Portions of this book originally appeared in *Steroid Abuse* by Tamara L. Roleff.

LUCENT PRESS

Published in 2017 by
Lucent Press, an Imprint of Greenhaven Publishing, LLC
353 3rd Avenue
Suite 255
New York, NY 10010

Designer: Deanna Paternostro
Editor: Jennifer Lombardo

Cataloging-in-Publication Data

Names: Rizzieri, Jordan.
Title: Steroids and other performance-enhancing drugs / Jordan Rizzieri.
Description: New York : Lucent Press, 2017. | Series: Drug education library| Includes index.
Identifiers: ISBN 9781534560031 (library bound) | ISBN 9781534560048 (ebook)
Subjects: LCSH: Anabolic steroids–Juvenile literature. | Steroid abuse–Juvenile literature. | Doping in sports–Juvenile literature.
Classification: LCC RC1230.R59 2017 | DDC 362.29'9–dc23

Printed in the United States of America

CPSIA compliance information: Batch #CW17KL: For further information contact Greenhaven Publishing LLC, New York, New York at 1-844-317-7404.

Please visit our website, www.greenhavenpublishing.com. For a free color catalog of all our high-quality books, call toll free 1-844-317-7404 or fax 1-844-317-7405.

Contents

Foreword

The development of drugs and drug use in America is a cultural paradox. On the one hand, strong, potentially dangerous drugs provide people with relief from numerous physical and psychological ailments. Sedatives like Valium counter the effects of anxiety; steroids treat severe burns, anemia, and some forms of cancer; morphine provides quick pain relief. On the other hand, many drugs (sedatives, steroids, and morphine among them) are consistently misused or abused. Millions of Americans struggle each year with drug addictions that overpower their ability to think and act rationally. Researchers often link drug abuse to criminal activity, traffic accidents, domestic violence, and suicide.

These harmful effects seem obvious today. Newspaper articles, medical papers, and scientific studies have highlighted the myriad problems drugs and drug use can cause. Yet, there was a time when many of the drugs now known to be harmful were actually believed to be beneficial. Cocaine, for example, was once hailed as a great cure, used to treat everything from nausea and weakness to colds and asthma. Developed in Europe during the 1880s, cocaine spread quickly to the United States, where manufacturers made it the primary ingredient in such everyday substances as cough medicines, lozenges, and tonics. Likewise, heroin, an opium derivative, became a popular painkiller during the late nineteenth century. Doctors and patients flocked to American drugstores to buy heroin, described as the optimal cure for even the worst coughs and chest pains.

As more people began using these drugs, though, doctors, legislators, and the public at large began to realize that they were more damaging than beneficial. After years of using heroin as a painkiller, for example, patients began asking their doctors for larger and stronger doses. Cocaine users reported dangerous side effects, including hallucinations and wild mood shifts. As a result, the U.S. government initiated more stringent regulation of many powerful and addictive drugs, and in some cases outlawed them entirely.

A drug's legal status is not always indicative of how dangerous it is, however. Some drugs known to have harmful effects can be purchased legally in the United States and elsewhere. Nicotine, a key ingredient in cigarettes, is known to be highly addictive. In an effort to meet their bodies' demands for nicotine, smokers expose themselves to lung cancer, emphysema, and other life-threatening conditions. Despite these risks, nicotine is legal almost everywhere.

Other drugs that cannot be purchased or sold legally are the subject of much debate regarding their effects on physical and mental health. Marijuana, sometimes described as a gateway drug that leads users to other drugs, cannot legally be used, grown, or sold in half of the United States. However, some research suggests that marijuana is neither addictive nor a gateway drug and that it might actually have a host of health benefits, which has led to its legalization in many states for medical use only. A handful of states also permit it to be used recreationally, but the debate on this matter still rages.

The Drug Education Library examines the paradox of drugs and drug use in America by focusing on some of the most commonly used and abused drugs or categories of drugs available today. By discussing objectively the many types of drugs, their intended purposes, their effects (both planned and unplanned), and the controversies surrounding them, the books in this series provide readers with an understanding of the complex role drugs and drug use play in American society. Informative sidebars, annotated bibliographies, and organizations to contact lists highlight the text and provide young readers with many opportunities for further discussion and research.

AN ORGANIZATION'S EPIDEMIC

Major League Baseball (MLB) was shocked when a scandal involving seven current MLB players broke in 2013. A previous employee of Biogenesis of America released documents to the *Miami Herald* newspaper stating the clinic had been a front for providing several players with performance-enhancing drugs such as testosterone and human growth hormone (HGH). All of the named individuals were subsequently suspended for 50 or more games, with the most lengthy and notable of suspensions going to American League All-Star, MVP, and Silver Slugger award winner, New York Yankees third baseman Alex Rodriguez.

Taking It Seriously

Major League Baseball was one of the last sporting organizations to crack down on players who use performance-enhancing drugs (PEDs). The steroid androstenedione was discovered in Mark McGwire's locker during his home run race with Sammy Sosa in 1998, but no action was taken against him because steroid use was not banned in baseball at the time. After an anonymous survey of drug use among ballplayers in 2003 showed that 5 to 7 percent of baseball players used steroids, MLB finally banned steroids and performance-enhancing substances and enacted drug testing policies. Players who tested positive for steroids in 2004 were sent to a counselor. The following year, ballplayers were given a 10-game suspension, and 12 players—including Rafael Palmeiro, who five months earlier had testified before Congress, "I have never used steroids. Period."[1]—were suspended. In 2006 the suspension policy was changed again, this time to 50 games.

Alex Rodriguez, pictured here, was suspended for the entire 2014 season (162 games plus postseason play) after MLB discovered his steroid use amid the Biogenesis scandal.

Saving Face

Ten years prior to the Biogenesis scandal, *Sports Illustrated* magazine revealed that Alex Rodriguez was one of 104 ballplayers who had tested positive for steroids in 2003. At first Rodriguez refused to confirm or deny the allegations, saying, "You'll have to talk to the union."[2] At the time Rodriguez failed this drug test, Major League Baseball prohibited players from using illegal drugs, including steroids, but did not have penalties in place for those who tested positive for drugs. A few days after his positive test result was leaked, Rodriguez admitted in an ESPN interview that he had been taking steroids during the years he had played for Texas. Rodriguez explained he felt pressure to live up to the standards expected of him and added: "Back then, [baseball] was a different culture. It was very loose. I was young. I was stupid.

I was naïve. And I wanted to prove to everyone that I was worth being one of the greatest players of all time. I did take a banned substance. And for that, I am very sorry and deeply regretful."[3]

Following Rodriguez's admission and apology, he began work with the Taylor Hooton Foundation, a nonprofit organization that teaches kids about the dangers of steroid use. Then, the *Miami Herald* released an article in November 2014 stating Rodriguez had admitted his PED use to the Drug Enforcement Administration in order to gain immunity against federal prosecution. In an interview with ESPN.com, the president of the foundation, Don Hooton Sr., said he was "very, very disappointed but not surprised" about Rodriguez's confession. "If his admission is accurate, his messages to kids about learning his lesson and playing performance-enhancing-drug free were disingenuous to say the least."[4]

Behind the Scenes

In his second book about steroids in baseball, *Vindicated: Big Names, Big Liars, and the Battle to Save Baseball,* former professional ballplayer and admitted steroid user Jose Canseco disputed Major League Baseball's figures of 5 to 7 percent steroid use among ballplayers. According to Canseco, in the whole clubhouse—indeed, practically the whole league—at least "80 percent or more"[5] took steroids. Canseco wrote of injecting steroids into McGwire, Palmeiro, Juan Gonzalez, and Ivan Rodriguez, to name just a few. The atmosphere in the locker room was so loose and casual, Canseco wrote, that the ballplayers would talk candidly about which steroids they used and in what dosages. According to Canseco, "This was light conversation, and we never bothered to stop unless a reporter was around. By 1997, in front of anyone but the media, it was completely accepted that we would talk openly about steroids."[6]

Canseco claimed it is easy to determine who is using steroids. Ballplayers who suddenly bulk up and weigh 40 pounds (18 kg) more at spring training than they did the previous fall are obvious candidates for steroid use, he asserted. Statistics could also be a telltale sign. Barry Bonds, who had hit 49 home runs in

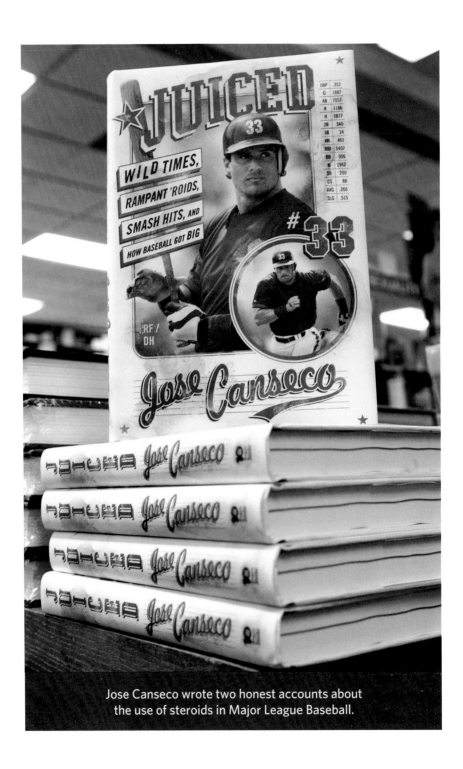

OBP	.353
G	1887
AB	7057
R	1186
H	1877
2B	340
3B	14
HR	462
RBI	1407
BB	906
K	1942
SB	200
CS	88
AVG	.266
SLG	.515

Jose Canseco wrote two honest accounts about the use of steroids in Major League Baseball.

2000, hit a record-breaking 73 home runs the following season after beginning to take steroids at the end of 2000, according to Canseco. Other ballplayers also posted impressive improvements to their stats. Mark McGwire hit 39 home runs in 1995, 58 in 1997, and 70 in 1998. Sammy Sosa was close to doubling the number of home runs he hit in just one year, going from 36 home runs in 1997 to 66 in 1998.

One of the arguments against steroid use is that if a few players take steroids, then everyone will need to use steroids to remain competitive. According to Canseco and others like him, players needed to take these performance-enhancing substances in order to keep their jobs. Canseco said it was because he and a few other baseball stars started taking steroids that 80 percent or more of ballplayers ended up using performance-enhancing drugs. It became, he said, "the Steroid Era."[7]

Chapter One

PERFORMANCE-ENHANCING DRUGS IN SPORTS: A HISTORY

To find out how serious the problem of steroid use in baseball was, Baseball Commissioner Bud Selig asked former senator George J. Mitchell to study the issue. Mitchell released his report in December 2007, and he named nearly 90 current and former baseball players who used steroids. In the report, Mitchell explained that a ballplayer's use of performance-enhancing drugs raises questions about whether or not baseball is being presented dishonestly to its fan base, and that all aspects of the league, from the owners and coaches to the union officials and trainers, are part of the problem. When any major league sports organization continues to demand increasingly high levels of performance, and seemingly rewards those who use steroids to achieve the lofty goals set before them, it "unfairly disadvantages the honest athletes who refuse to use them and raises questions about the validity of baseball records."[8] By the time anyone in Major League Baseball realized how extensive steroid use was in the organization and how dangerous it was to the well-being of the players, it had already become quietly synonymous with outstanding performance, making it deeply entangled in the careers of many ballplayers. At Mitchell's urging, baseball officials made drastic changes to their policies regarding performance-enhancing drugs and began to more thoroughly investigate allegations of steroid use. The league developed a comprehensive education program for players about the health risks of steroids and performance-enhancing drugs and incorporated year-round, random, unannounced drug testing. They concluded that the first step to gaining a sport

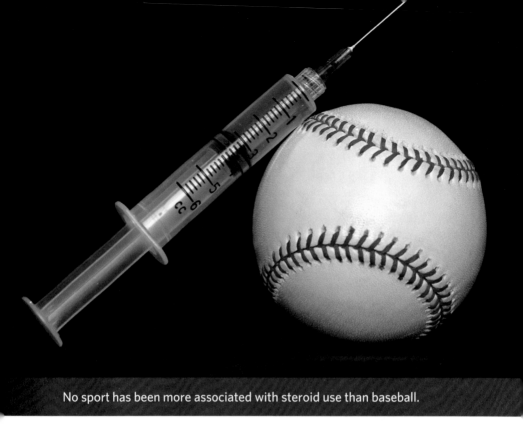

No sport has been more associated with steroid use than baseball.

without steroids and performance-enhancing substances was to take such drug use seriously, adopting and upholding strict policies.

Major League Baseball is not the first, and certainly not the only, sport that has had to assess the steroid and PED use of its players. Steroid use dates back more than 60 years in professional sports, after medical discoveries showed they could stimulate muscle development and increase stamina. Scientifically, a steroid is a naturally-occurring, complex hormone found in the human body; estrogen and testosterone are two examples. Anabolic-androgenic steroids, commonly referred to simply as "steroids," are synthetic, or manmade, versions of naturally-produced hormones that build up tissues, particularly muscles, bones, and red blood cells, while stimulating the development of male sexual characteristics, such as body hair, a deep voice, and aggressiveness. Testosterone, a commonly used steroid, was isolated by scientists in the 1930s and used to treat medical conditions such as delayed puberty in males. Once testosterone was isolated, it was relatively easy for scientists to find other steroids and synthesize them in the laboratory.

Amphetamines

Amphetamines are drugs that stimulate the nervous system, raise blood pressure, increase energy, and speed up the heart rate. One type of amphetamine is methamphetamine, or meth—a highly addictive drug that was used by the Allies, Nazis, and Japanese during World War II to keep soldiers awake for long periods of time. Later, it was prescribed as a diet drug because it increases the rate at which the body burns calories. Today, meth is illegal due to its dangerous side effects, which include anxiety, paranoia, mood swings, sores, and rotting teeth. It is easy to die from an overdose of meth because it is made in batches in illegal laboratories. The ingredients and strength may change from batch to batch, so it is difficult for a meth user to know exactly what they are taking and in what amounts.

Amphetamine, although closely related to meth, has fewer negative side effects. It can be addictive and cause depression, anxiety, and irrational behavior. However, in small doses prescribed by a doctor, it has a positive effect on people with attention deficit hyperactivity disorder (ADHD). Adderall is the most commonly prescribed amphetamine for ADHD. It balances chemicals in the brain to help a person with ADHD concentrate and calm down, but people without this chemical imbalance who take Adderall have more energy.

Amphetamine pills such as Adderall and dextroamphetamine sulphate—diet pills commonly known as "greenies" because the capsules were green and white—have been used as performance-enhancing drugs for decades. In the 1950s, people viewed amphetamine as a type of "miracle drug" that allowed them to lose weight and have more energy, so it was widely available. Greenies were especially popular in baseball because they gave players more energy, alertness, and better reaction time. Players would often get them from friends who had a doctor's prescription.

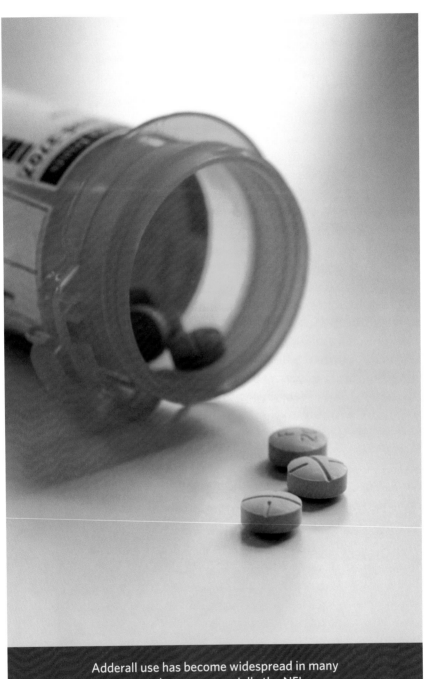

Adderall use has become widespread in many sports leagues, especially the NFL.

Doctors stopped prescribing most types of amphetamines by the 1970s, and Adderall is banned by the NFL, MLB, Major League Soccer, the National Collegiate Athletic Association (NCAA), and the Olympics. However, Adderall remains widely used and abused, especially in the NFL.

Steroids as Medical Treatment

Scientists and doctors were excited about the development of synthetic steroids because they could use them to treat many diseases and disorders. Because the effects of anabolic steroids are to build up muscles and bones, help bodies recover faster, increase the production of red blood cells, and increase feelings of well-being and energy, the Allies found them to be a great help in treating the starving prisoners in the Nazi concentration camps at the end of World War II. Anabolic steroids are also effective at treating people who suffer from cachexia, or wasting syndrome, due to AIDS or cancer. Jesse Haggard, a naturopathic doctor and author of the book *Demystifying Steroids*, writes that he prescribed steroids for a middle-aged patient who was wasting away due to a lack of appetite associated with the human immunodeficiency virus (HIV). After four weeks on steroids, the patient gained 15 pounds (6.8 kg) and "looked fantastically healthy."[9]

Because steroids are well known for stimulating muscle and tissue growth, they are also used to treat burn victims. Due to a drastic upset in the natural equilibrium of a human's internal processes, testosterone production slows and can stop completely in people with severe burns, causing a drastic loss of muscle mass. A study conducted at the Federal University of São Paulo in Brazil and published in 2014 found that burn patients who were given oxandrolone, a synthetic form of testosterone, had "lesser loss of corporal mass, lesser nitrogen loss, and shorter donor area healing time"[10] than those patients in the control group.

Steroids are used to stimulate bone marrow production as well. In a rare but extremely serious condition called Diamond-Blackfan anemia (DBA), the bone marrow does not produce enough red blood cells. Red blood cells carry oxygen to the tissues in the body; a lack of oxygen will cause the tissue to die. In one study, a large group of people with DBA were given steroids to stimulate their bone marrow into producing red blood cells. It was a very successful treatment; the bone marrow in 82 percent of the people responded to this treatment and began producing red blood cells. Today, corticosteroid therapy is a heavily utilized treatment for DBA, with about 79 percent of patients initially responding to the steroids.

Human growth hormone is another steroid that has been successfully used to treat medical conditions such as children's growth disorders and HGH deficiencies in adults. Growth hormone is an anabolic steroid that is produced in the pituitary gland. Children who have a deficiency of HGH grow noticeably slower than other children, and if not treated, they may be shorter than average, have poor bone and muscle development, have delayed eruption of teeth, may experience hypoglycemia (low blood sugar), and may experience gaps in the closures of the skull. Adults with growth hormone deficiency have decreased muscle and bone density, low energy, and are often obese. Treatment of children or adults with growth hormone deficiencies consists of raising the HGH levels to normal. Growth hormone given to children prior to puberty can accelerate their growth rate and increase muscle development. Growth hormone given after puberty will not have an effect on height because the bones have stopped growing. In adults, HGH builds muscles, increases energy, and reduces body fat.

Bodybuilding and Weight Lifting

After steroids were used successfully to treat those who were suffering from malnourishment during World War II, they became popular among athletes because of the effects they have on the body—building up muscles and increasing red blood cells. Trainers, coaches, and athletes found that if steroids were taken, the athletes were able to train harder, develop more muscle mass and

The history of athletic steroid use can be traced back to weight lifters in the early 1950s.

body strength, and increase their energy levels, all beyond what they would be able to accomplish without steroids.

The first documented use of steroids in athletic competition was during the 1952 Olympic Games in Helsinki, Finland. Weight lifters from the Soviet Union won seven medals, including three golds. The U.S. weight lifting coach, Bob Hoffman, told reporters, "I know they're taking the hormone stuff to increase their strength."[11] A Soviet team physician confirmed these suspicions two years later; he confessed to an American team physician, John Ziegler, at the World Weightlifting Championships in 1954, where the Soviets continued their domination of weight lifting.

While working with a pharmaceutical company, Ziegler developed an oral synthetic steroid for use in burn patients that replicated many of testosterone's muscle-building properties while reducing its negative side effects. The result was Dianabol, which was quickly adopted by Hoffman and members of his bodybuilding club in York, Pennsylvania.

The results were dramatic; the bodybuilders quickly bulked up while using the synthetic steroid. Hoffman tried to keep his bodybuilders' use a secret, claiming their impressive weight gains and beefy muscles were the result of a new training program he developed called isometric contraction. However, other bodybuilders were not able to duplicate the remarkable results—until they, too, discovered the 5-milligram tablets of Dianabol. By the 1960s, steroid use was commonplace among weight lifters and bodybuilders. Terry Todd, an elite weight lifter during the 1960s who used Dianabol, claimed that steroids, "combined with proper training and nutrition, are able to produce athletic benefits, at least in the short run."[12]

The Olympics

Soon athletes around the world began incorporating steroids into their training programs. In 1968, East Germany competed for the first time with its own teams of athletes at the Summer Olympic Games in Mexico City. East Germans won a total of 25 medals, including 9 gold. Four years later in Munich, East

Germany more than doubled its medal count with 66 medals, including 20 gold, coming in third behind the Soviet Union and the United States. According to Richard Pound, a member of the International Olympic Committee (IOC) and a founder of the World Anti-Doping Agency (WADA), "By the time of the Montreal Games in 1976, the question in women's swimming was not how many gold medals the East Germans would win, but whether anyone else could win any."[13] His question was not far off the mark; East German women won 10 gold medals in 12 events in women's swimming, and the East Germans again doubled the total number of gold medals they won: 40 gold, along

In the late 1960s and early 1970s, doping was widespread among Olympic athletes because many drug tests could not accurately detect the drugs the athletes were using.

HUMAN GROWTH HORMONE VERSUS STEROIDS

Anabolic steroids and human growth hormone (HGH) share some similarities, and many people believe that HGH is a steroid. However, there are several small but important differences between these two substances. One is that although steroids have testosterone in them, this naturally-occurring hormone is often changed slightly in a laboratory to produce different effects. This means athletes can choose one steroid to build muscle and another to reduce fat. Naturally-occurring testosterone does not give people these options. In contrast, HGH is exactly like the hormone that occurs naturally in the body to help children grow. It is created in a lab as well, but its chemical structure is not changed.

Because HGH is natural and steroids are not, HGH is absorbed better by the body with fewer side effects. HGH's side effects include nerve and muscle pain, numbness of the skin, and high levels of cholesterol. Both substances are used to build muscle and speed recovery time, although one study found that although HGH did increase lean body mass, it "did not produce measurable increases in either strength or exercise capacity."[1] Test subjects were also likely to get tired more quickly and retain fluid.

1. "Growth Hormone, Athletic Performance, and Aging," *Harvard Health Publications*, May 2010. www.health.harvard.edu/diseases-and-conditions/growth-hormone-athletic-performance-and-aging.

with 50 silver and bronze, second only to the Soviet Union in total medal count.

By this time it was suspected that East German athletes, especially the women swimmers, were doing something besides training to achieve such dramatic results. When a rival coach noted that the East German women swimmers had very deep voices, a telltale sign of steroid use in women, an East German coach responded, "We came here to swim, not sing."[14] While officials suspected the East Germans of doping their athletes, there were no tests at the time that could definitively prove the athletes were taking steroids, despite the fact that the IOC had begun testing athletes for drugs in 1968.

Track and Field

Quickly, athletes in other sports sought the results being seen in weight lifting, bodybuilding, and swimming. Athletes who used steroids were winning more competitions than those who stayed clean. In 1989, Charlie Francis, a coach for Olympic track and field star Ben Johnson, was compelled by the Canadian government to testify in what came to be known as the Dubin Inquiry about his role in Johnson testing positive for the steroid stanozolol at the 1988 Olympic Games. Francis stated that he was convinced all the top track and field athletes were taking steroids. "I couldn't find a single case where it appeared that performance-enhancing drugs were not being used,"[15] he testified. Francis said he had been giving his athletes performance-enhancing substances for almost a decade because they had to "break the rules or lose."[16] Charles Yesalis, an expert in performance-enhancing drugs, claimed that two-thirds of the athletes at the 1972 Olympics had used steroids at one time. According to Yesalis, the popular belief that athletes who take steroids "are only a few bad apples in the barrel" is false. In actuality, he said, "There's only a few good apples in the barrel."[17]

Adam Nelson, a shot putter who won the silver medal at the Olympics in Athens in 2004, claimed to be one of those good apples. In 2012, his claim was validated. More than 100 urine samples of Olympic athletes from that year's games were retested, and the test belonging to Yuriy Bilonog of Ukraine, who had beaten Nelson for gold in shot put, came up positive. He was subsequently stripped of his title, and Nelson's silver officially became gold in 2013. Nelson said, "There's just a massive

Shot-putter Adam Nelson (left) was rewarded for competing clean after his 2004 gold medal opponent tested positive for performance-enhancing drugs.

amount of misinformation that says the only way to improve performance substantially is through taking performance-enhancing drugs ... It used to frustrate the heck out of me—you can't throw this far or run this time or jump this far unless you do this."[18]

The NFL

Steroid use in professional football was first documented in 1962 to 1963, and according to the National Football League's (NFL) former drug adviser Forrest Tennant, "athletes openly took them,"[19] at least until steroids were banned by the NFL in 1983. A 2008 report by the *San Diego Union-Tribune*, in which 185 NFL players are named as having taken performance-enhancing drugs, is not even considered to be a comprehensive list of players who used such drugs. "It is believed to only scratch the surface of actual usage in pro football,"[20] the paper asserted. Yesalis maintained that the names listed in the report were just "the tip of the iceberg."[21] The report claimed that entire football teams used steroids in the 1960s and 1970s and that the actual number of players who used steroids and other performance-enhancing drugs could number in the thousands, of which only a very tiny percentage were ever caught.

Steroid Use in Cycling

Like football teams of the 1960s and 1970s, entire teams of professional cyclists have been caught using steroids and other performance-enhancing substances during major races, notably the Tour de France. In 2006, this three-week cycling race was plagued with doping scandals. Favored cyclists Jan Ullrich of Germany and Ivan Basso of Italy were expelled from the race after their names were linked to Eufemiano Fuentes, a Spanish doctor who was accused of administering banned substances to more than 200 athletes. In addition, two Spanish cycling teams were forced to withdraw from the race due to their involvement with Fuentes. American Floyd Landis had his win stripped from him after a drug test found abnormal levels of testosterone in his system. The 2007 Tour de France was practically a repeat of the year before; five cyclists and two teams were dismissed or withdrew from the race for failing drug tests. Greg LeMond, an American who won the Tour de France three times in the 1980s, said that performance-enhancing substances give the cyclist an unfair advantage. "Doping increases a cyclist's capacity 30 percent. At the top form of my career, I could not have finished in the leading 15 in the Tour today [because of the use of steroids in the sport],"[22] he told a French newspaper in 2007. In 2008, nine members of the Portuguese cycling team were suspended after officials found banned substances and doping equipment in the team's headquarters.

The Downfall of Lance Armstrong

Lance Armstrong had one of the most decorated careers in cycling history. Not only did he win seven consecutive Tour de France victories from 1999 to 2005, he also beat stage three testicular cancer, even after the cancer had spread to other parts of his body, including his brain. By the fall of 2012, after more than a decade of allegations fueled by competitors and people close to Armstrong, an investigation by the United States Anti-Doping Agency (USADA) was opened. The USADA ruled that Armstrong was in fact guilty of using erythropoietin, or EPO—a hormone that increases red blood cell count in order to transport more oxygen to muscles, improving performance and stamina. This practice is sometimes called "blood doping."

In January 2013, the world tuned in to watch in shock as Armstrong admitted to interviewer Oprah Winfrey that he had, in fact, used EPO and other banned substances to successfully achieve his Tour de France record. Subsequently, Armstrong was stripped of all seven of his Tour de France victories as well as his bronze medal from the 2000 Olympics. WADA also ruled that Armstrong be banned for life from all sports that fall under their jurisdiction.

Major League Baseball

Major League Baseball was one of the last professional sport organizations to ban performance-enhancing drugs. Ken Caminiti, who was named the National League's Most Valuable Player in 1996, admitted to *Sports Illustrated* that he was a heavy user of steroids during his MVP year. He told the magazine that steroid use was common in baseball: "It's no secret what's going on

Lance Armstrong was stripped of his seven Tour de France victories and banned for life from competitive cycling after he admitted to doping.

in baseball. At least half the guys are using steroids. They talk about it. They joke about it with each other."[23] Jose Canseco, who played baseball for 16 years in the major leagues, wrote in his book *Juiced* that the majority of ballplayers used steroids: "If I had to guess, I'd say eight out of every ten players had kits in their lockers filled with growth hormones, steroids, supplements—you name it."[24]

THE RUSSIAN GOVERNMENT'S ROLE IN DOPING

When an Olympic medal is at stake, some governments are willing to do anything to help their country's teams win. In 2016, Grigory Rodchenkov, the former director of a Russian drug testing laboratory that provided drug tests for Olympic athletes, confessed that he had helped the Russian government give athletes banned substances and cover up the evidence before the 2014 Olympic Games:

In a dark-of-night operation, Russian antidoping experts and members of the intelligence service surreptitiously replaced urine samples tainted by performance-enhancing drugs with clean urine collected months earlier, somehow breaking into the supposedly tamper-proof bottles that are the standard at international competitions, Dr. Rodchenkov said. For hours each night, they worked in a shadow laboratory lit by a single lamp, passing bottles of urine through a hand-size hole in the wall, to be ready for testing the next day, he said.[1]

Rodchenkov estimated that about 100 samples were replaced. No athletes were caught, and the Russians won most of the games they competed in at the 2014 Winter Games in Sochi. The athletes who had taken the drugs were banned from the 2016 Summer Games in Rio after Rodchenkov confessed.

1. Rebecca R. Ruiz and Michael Schwirtz, "Russian Insider Says State-Run Doping Fueled Olympic Gold," *New York Times*, May 12, 2016. www.nytimes.com/2016/05/13/sports/russia-doping-sochi-olympics-2014.html.

MLB started cracking down on players who tested positive for steroids after the findings of the Mitchell Report in 2007. In May 2009, it suspended Manny Ramirez of the Los Angeles Dodgers for 50 games when he tested positive for human chorionic gonadotropin, a banned performance enhancer that is used to stimulate testosterone production after finishing a cycle of steroid drugs. As of MLB's 2015 Joint Drug Prevention and Treatment Program, the organization has banned 138 substances, 74 of which fall under the heading of performance-enhancing drugs. The penalty for testing positive for such substances is now an 80-game suspension for the first offense, 162 games for the second, and permanent suspension for the third.

The Dangers of Steroid Use

While athletes are willing to take steroids and other performance-enhancing drugs to further their abilities in sports, they might not be considering the other effects the drugs are having on their bodies. When any drug, whether it is an illegal substance or something prescribed by a doctor, is introduced to the body, it alters the homeostasis of the body's systems. Homeostasis is the equilibrium, or balance, inside the body. When a new substance enters the body and alters its chemical balance, the effects can be as positive as clearing up infections or as negative as the deterioration of major organs. While experiencing perceived positive effects of steroids and PEDs, such as increased stamina and muscle mass, athletes may be unaware of what else is being negatively affected inside their bodies.

Chapter Two

EFFECTS ON THE BODY

Despite state and federal laws restricting steroids, athletes who really want them can generally find a source easily. Steroids are still legal with or without a prescription in many other countries, most notably Mexico, Thailand, Poland, and Colombia. Moreover, numerous websites sell steroids online, although many of the steroids are counterfeit or fake. Like adults, most teens have no problem buying steroids over the Internet. "It was a ... piece of cake," said Joe P., a teen in south Florida. "I had the [steroids] delivered right to my parents' house."[25] Steroids are often sold on the black market at gyms, competitions, sometimes from coaches and trainers, and occasionally from doctors, pharmacists, and veterinarians. (Steroids used for animals are often the same as or similar to those used on humans.) For those who are chemically inclined, the raw ingredients may be purchased and combined to produce homemade versions of anabolic steroids.

Steroids bought in foreign countries, on the black market, or from veterinarians present even more dangers to users than the potential adverse side effects. These drugs are often not made with the same degree of quality control, and they are sometimes produced in unsterile and unsanitary environments.

Use Versus Abuse

Steroids are drugs that must be prescribed by a doctor. Like other drugs, they have positive and negative effects on the body. Taken properly and under a doctor's orders, low doses

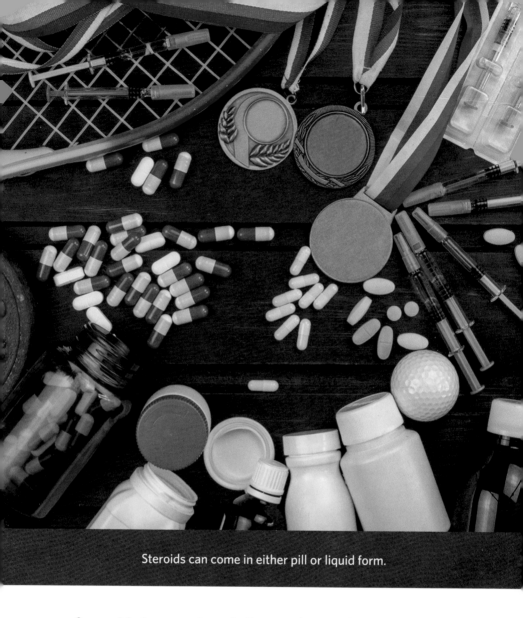

Steroids can come in either pill or liquid form.

of steroid drugs reduce inflammation and provide pain relief due to arthritis, bursitis, and tendonitis; stimulate appetites; and help build up muscles and other tissues that have wasted away due to diseases such as cancer or AIDS. However, athletes who use steroids to help them build up muscles use doses that are higher than recommended, and these doses can cause dangerous and irreversible side effects.

Steroids are generally taken either orally, in pill form, or injected. Athletes tend to take several different types of steroids at the same time in a process called stacking. For example, one steroid is used as the base to build muscle mass, another steroid may be used to promote tissue and muscle recovery after workouts, and a third steroid may be used to increase body strength. Athletes typically start with a low dose of steroids, building up the amount over a period of several weeks. Then these athletes begin a period of reducing the doses, while adding other steroids and supplements. This process of taking increasing and decreasing doses of steroids is called cycling. An entire cycle may last 12 to 18 weeks. During a cycle, or in between cycles, athletes often forgo taking steroids for a couple of weeks. Some steroids are effective for only a few weeks at a time; some steroids are toxic to the liver or other organs when taken long term; and some steroids may stop the body from being able to produce testosterone or may cause it to produce an excess of the female hormone estrogen. It is during these down times that athletes will take other supplements to help the body recover from the steroids and help it start producing its own hormones again. Then after a few weeks off, the athlete starts the cycle all over again.

While steroids are used over a longer time period to change the way the body works in the long term—for instance, by building more muscle or reducing healing time—amphetamine is typically taken immediately before a game. The effects wear off when the pill does; depending on whether the player is using immediate-release or extended-release Adderall, this can be anywhere from 4 to 12 hours. This means taking the pill farther in advance is useless because the effects would wear off before the game.

People who have ADHD often genuinely need Adderall because it helps them concentrate on important tasks. Therefore, most sports leagues allow a therapeutic use exemption for players with ADHD if they have a doctor's prescription and have been evaluated by a league official to see whether they truly need that prescription.

The Immediate Downside: Side Effects

As with any drug, steroids come with side effects. These are secondary, generally unwanted results of steroid use that can be uncomfortable, embarrassing, a hindrance, and in some cases, dangerous.

Changes to the skin are a typical sign of steroid abuse. Androgenic steroids stimulate the sebaceous glands, which secrete oils in the skin. The excessive secretion of oils can cause rampant acne on the back, shoulders, and chest, and occasionally on the face. While dermatologists may be able to prescribe ointments to treat the acne, many of the scars and changes to the skin are permanent.

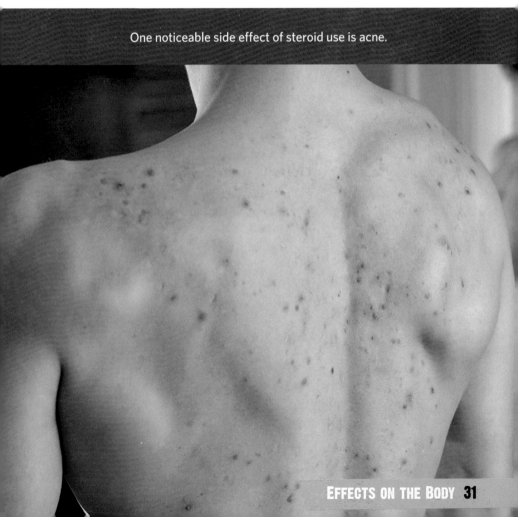

One noticeable side effect of steroid use is acne.

Some steroids also contribute to the development of gynecomastia, or the development of breasts in men. The body has an enzyme called aromatase that converts excess testosterone from steroids into estrogen, the female hormone, and estrogen is responsible for developing breast tissue. In addition, an excess of estrogen will stop the production of testosterone, which will lead to shrunken testicles. Dan Clark, who played the gladiator Nitro on the television show *American Gladiator*, injured his knee playing football in his freshman year of junior college. During rehabilitation after knee surgery, he dropped from 210 pounds (95 kg) down to a scrawny 178 pounds (81 kg). A friend at his gym told him about steroids and how they would help him get his strength back in a hurry. Clark saw a doctor who prescribed two steroids for him, Dianabol and testosterone cypionate. Warned about the side effects, Clark said he was more worried that the steroids would not work for him, a worry that turned out to be groundless. He said, "The steroids don't just work, they are everything the doctor said they would be, and more. I'm surprised by how fast my body responds to the drugs. One day I'm benching 185, the next, 225. I get big, ripped, and strong, and I gain back all the weight I lost from surgery, plus an additional ten pounds."[26] Clark was elated by the changes in his body brought on by steroids, especially when he earned the Most Valuable Player award during his sophomore year and a scholarship to play football at a state college.

However, ignoring his doctor's warnings turned out to have devastating effects on his body, as Clark wrote in his tell-all book, *Gladiator*:

As a result of twenty years of steroid use, I walk with a limp, I have seven scars on my face, two destroyed knees, and I can't walk up a flight of stairs until I chug a couple of cups of black coffee and a handful of anti-inflammatory pills. What strapping eighteen-year-old athlete could ever imagine ending up with a herniated back disk and a neck that pops like fireworks on the Fourth of July from a mere turn of my head? And those are the obvious problems. The real prizes are a pair of shrunken testicles and surgical scars across my nipples from having breast tissue removed from my chest.[27]

Internal Effects

Unlike steroids, amphetamine does not change the appearance of the body. However, it does have dangerous internal side effects. An athlete's increased speed and endurance come with a cost: short-term and long-term effects. In the short term, users may experience "nervousness, restlessness … dizziness, headache … anxiety, agitation, tremor [shaking], weakness, blurred vision, sleep problems (insomnia),"[28] and more. Users may also find that they are more likely to get angry while they are taking Adderall. The drug is addictive, so someone who starts using it may have trouble stopping because they find that they cannot function on a daily basis without it. Over time, Adderall abuse can lead to weight loss and heart disease.

Steroids also have dangerous internal side effects. These involve major organs: the liver, the kidneys, and the prostate gland. The liver turns food into energy and nutrients while filtering out what cannot be metabolized. The prolonged use of some steroids has been shown to cause severe liver damage and development of blood-filled cysts on the liver and has been linked to liver cancer. The kidneys filter unwanted substances from the blood and create urine, which is then sent to the bladder. Steroid use is also linked to kidney tumors, and, especially if the athlete has high blood pressure, kidney damage. The prostate is a gland located below the bladder in men and helps to facilitate fertility. The abuse of testosterone is linked to an enlarged prostate, which often precedes prostate cancer, which is currently the second leading cause of cancer-related deaths in American men.

Altering the levels of hormones in the body can also cause depression and mood swings. In addition, high testosterone

Healthy

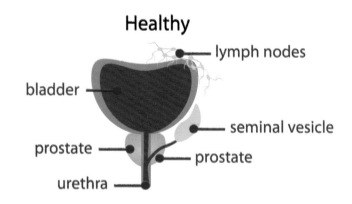

- lymph nodes
- bladder
- seminal vesicle
- prostate
- prostate
- urethra

Stages of prostate cancer

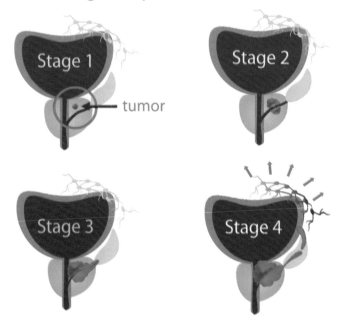

Stage 1 — tumor

Stage 2

Stage 3

Stage 4

Steroid use has been linked to an increased risk of prostate cancer.

levels are linked to aggressiveness. An athlete who increases his or her testosterone level through steroids is also increasing his or her feelings of aggression. While increased aggressiveness allows some athletes to train harder and longer, others cannot cope with their feelings and become easily irritated, impatient, and prone to angry outbursts. These symptoms are referred to as 'roid rage. Some athletes and body builders are suspected of killing their family members and themselves during periods of 'roid rage.

Effects on Women

Steroid use is not confined to men. The number of women athletes who use steroids has also grown dramatically, especially during the past few years. Side effects from using steroids—many of which are androgenic, or muscle builders—affect men and women differently. In addition, many of the side effects take a while to appear for men, but happen much more quickly for women. Gynecomastia in men may take more than one cycle to appear, and will generally disappear (or at least diminish) when the male athlete discontinues steroid use. The changes in women, however, often occur during their first cycle of steroid use. When on steroids, a woman's voice deepens, facial hair increases, and other physical changes take place. Many of these changes are permanent; for instance, a woman's voice that has changed due to steroid use will not change back to a more feminine register.

Steroids and Pregnancy

Because steroids are synthetic sex hormones, women who take steroids are at risk of permanently damaging their reproductive systems. Their menstrual cycles may slow or even stop, and the steroids may even make them infertile. Unlike men, women's infertility due to steroid abuse can often be permanent. More importantly, a woman who takes steroids while pregnant is risking the health of her unborn child. The abnormally high levels of steroids in a woman's body during

Being Led Astray

A common excuse heard from athletes who are accused of doping is that they were taking supplements given to them by their coach or trainer without knowing what they were taking. Many athletes and their coaches ordered legal supplements and—if they had the right connections—illegal performance-enhancing steroids from the Bay Area Laboratory Co-Operative (BALCO) in the San Francisco area. A grand jury called baseball player Barry Bonds to testify about BALCO and his personal steroid use. Bonds claimed they were not steroids but supplements and that he never asked his trainer about them. "When he said it was flaxseed oil, I just said, 'Whatever.' It was in the ballpark … in front of everybody. I mean, all the reporters, my teammates. I mean, they all saw it. I didn't hide it … You know, trainers come up to me and say, 'Hey Barry, try this.'" Then Bonds was asked if his trainer "came to you at the ballpark with some other substance, whatever it is, if he asked you to take some other substance and said it was some other type of oil, whatever he asked you to take, would you take it?" Bonds answered, "I would trust that he wouldn't do anything to hurt me." The prosecutor pressed Bonds on this issue, asking him again, "Okay. But you wouldn't ask any further questions. You'd just basically—because he's your friend, if he asked you to take it, you would take it?" Bonds replied, "He would do the same thing for me."[1]

1. Barry Bonds, 2003 Grand Jury Testimony, December 4, 2003. mlb.mlb.com/mlb/news/bonds030208.pdf.

pregnancy can cause intellectual disabilities or the development of both male and female sexual organs (called intersex) in her fetus.

A study of 52 Olympic athletes from East Germany—who were told the steroids they were systematically given by their trainers during the 1960s and 1970s were vitamins—found that their children had a much higher rate of serious medical issues than the general population. The athletes lost 15 children due to miscarriage, and three were stillborn, a rate 32 times higher than the normal German population. Giselher Spitzer, the study's author, found that the 69 children who survived had much higher rates than the general population of physical and mental handicaps, allergies, and asthma. "Children of mothers who were drugged

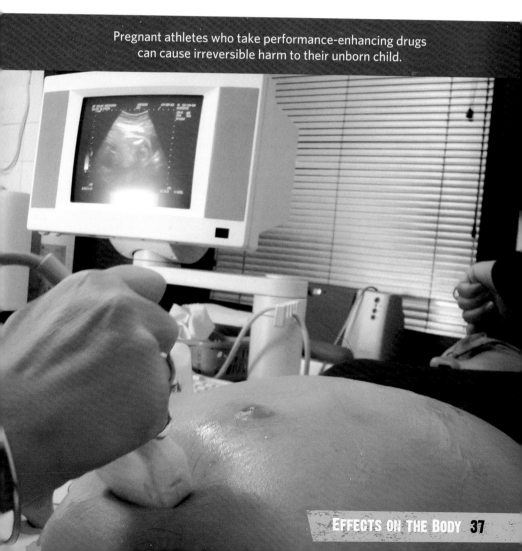

Pregnant athletes who take performance-enhancing drugs can cause irreversible harm to their unborn child.

typically suffer more from multiple handicaps than children of drugged fathers," Spitzer said at a 2007 conference on sport and society, and added, "54 percent of the children suffer from two illnesses."[29] He concluded that taking steroids is dangerous for everyone involved. "Your children will be damaged by that practice, and many athletes ... say 'It is my body and I'll do what I want.' It is not the truth, it's not only your body, it is the second generation, and we don't know what will be of the third generation."[30]

There are many reasons why people take steroids. Used properly, steroids will build muscle, increase muscle strength, and speed recovery time after workouts. Few users are completely educated about how to use steroids properly, however, and so they risk experiencing dangerous side effects from the drugs. Scientists and health professionals still do not know all the effects long-term steroid use has on the body.

Role Models for Teens

Because athletes are often considered role models who are idolized by teens and children, many people worry about the effect steroid use by athletes will have on youth. They fear that because athletes use steroids, teens will try to emulate their heroes and use steroids as well. According to Bernard Griesemer, an expert on steroid use in teen athletes, and the author of the American Academy of Pediatrics's position paper on steroids, "What athletes wear, do, say, and take have a huge impact on your young athletes."[31] That influence, he said, includes steroid use. If athletic superstars are using steroids, it is more likely that young athletes will emulate their heroes and use steroids, too.

The 2016 Monitoring the Future survey had encouraging news about teens and steroids. Steroid use among eighth, tenth, and twelfth graders had decreased for the past decade. According to the survey, 0.9 percent of 8th graders and 1.3 percent of 10th graders had ever used steroids, while 1.6 percent of 12th graders had used steroids, all of which were decreases in usage over the past

THE MEDIA AND THE STEROID LOOK

It is not just athletes hoping to gain strength and power who use steroids. Teens, specifically teen boys, are overwhelmed by images of muscular bodies, according to Linn Goldberg, the cofounder of ATLAS and ATHENA, two programs that educate teen athletes about proper nutrition and the dangers of steroid use. He testified before Congress about how the media shapes teens' ideas about their bodies, saying:

The media influences teens [when] ... hyper-muscular pictures are frequently on the cover of many magazines. Children's items and images from GI Joe figures to comic strip characters have had a "steroidal" makeover, reflecting unrealistic muscular body types. The advertising tactic using the term "on steroids" is often used to market products that include automobiles, software, negotiating seminars, notepads and running shoes. This strategy suggests that their product is so superb, it is similar to being on steroids.[1]

1. Linn Goldberg, Testimony Before the U.S. House of Representatives, Committee on Government Reform, April 27, 2005. oversight.house.gov/documents/20050 427111957-63760.pdf.

decade. However, the Centers for Disease Control and Prevention's 2015 Youth Risk Behavior Survey found that 3.5 percent of 9th through 12th graders had used steroids at least once in their lives, although that percentage had fallen from a high of 6.1 percent in 2003.

Like other surveys of steroid use, accurate counts of college athletes who use steroids and other performance-enhancing drugs are notoriously hard to get. One early study found that 20 percent of college athletes had used steroids by 1984, but according to the NCAA, steroid use has fallen dramatically

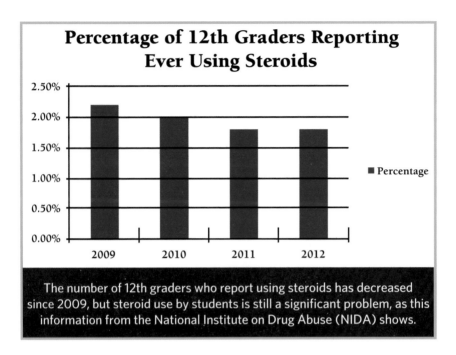

Percentage of 12th Graders Reporting Ever Using Steroids

■ Percentage

2009 2010 2011 2012

The number of 12th graders who report using steroids has decreased since 2009, but steroid use by students is still a significant problem, as this information from the National Institute on Drug Abuse (NIDA) shows.

since then. Drug tests and penalties for positive results seem to have a deterrent effect on steroid use. Drug tests reveal that the number of college athletes who have tested positive for banned substances has fallen to 3 percent. In 1986, the NCAA started testing college athletes for drugs and steroids before championship games. When Brian Bosworth, a linebacker for the University of Oklahoma, and two of his teammates tested positive for steroids that year, the NCAA ruled they were ineligible to play in the Orange Bowl.

Pressures from the Outside

High school students are more likely to use steroids as a result of peer pressure than older athletes. The desire not to appear different from their peers can strongly affect behavior. Moreover, if other athletes are using steroids, some teens may feel they have to take steroids to be competitive.

Coaches also may influence athletes to take steroids—inadvertently or deliberately—by making comments about the athletes' body or size. "Comments such as 'You could stand to gain a few extra pounds,' or 'If you were bigger you could play on the team,' send a message,"[32] said Joseph Berning, an exercise physiologist and professor at New Mexico State University. Some student athletes, especially those who feel pressure to perform well so they will be selected to play a sport for college or professional teams, may feel pressure to use steroids to get big and strong fast. The lure of lucrative contracts and salaries encourages some to use steroids

Men and women who are not athletes sometimes take steroids in an effort to achieve society's "ideal" body type.

to enhance their records and statistics. Kris Castellanos, who played baseball at Florida State University, explained why many college athletes decide to use steroids. "Guys are thinking that's pretty much the only way to get there or that's the easiest way to get where they want to."[33]

High school students also take steroids to look good for the opposite sex, rather than trying to bulk up for a sport. Dionne Roberts was 17 years old and a high school cheerleader and gymnast. She wanted to look toned, to have that look of "six-pack abs,"[34] as she described it, so she started taking steroids. She said, "It's not uncommon to strive for that four-pack or six-pack, even in girls. Being in shape is not just a masculine thing." She said she was influenced to use steroids by the images she saw on television and in the movies. "It's this whole Hollywood thing," she said. "Everyone is so affected by movie stars and that whole pop culture thing. I think it takes over a little bit. We have to get back to reality. Everybody has their own quarrels with self-esteem and self-image, and that's what every young woman goes through."[35]

Wanting to Look Good

Teens are not the only ones who use steroids to improve their image or who want to bulk up and get bigger. Personal trainers, models, dancers, and movie stars, as well as some firefighters, police officers, and military service members, use steroids because they want to change their body image by bulking up or developing their muscles. Some may want to change their bodies because they want to perform better in their chosen sport or profession, while others just want to look fit and muscular. Adolescents and teens often become preoccupied with their body and body image. Insecurities about fitting in with their peers and looking desirable to members of the opposite sex may lead some teens to try steroids. One young man said he bought some steroid pills at his gym to look better for women:

DO DRUGS HAVE A PLACE IN CYCLING?

Some people believe there is no way to ever completely eliminate performance-enhancing drugs from sports. Simply because fewer people are failing drug tests than in the past does not necessarily mean that fewer people are doping, just that they may be more careful about it now. For that reason, some argue, it is better to allow those drugs so their use can be more closely monitored. Professor Julian Savulescu, who shares this view when it comes to cycling, suggested that instead, drugs that can already be found in the human body should be allowed and tested to be sure the athlete is not using an unhealthy amount. The drugs Savulescu would approve include EPO, HGH, and testosterone; he would still support banning painkillers and anti-inflammatory drugs because he believes an important part of sports is being able to deal with pain.

Savulescu feels that allowing cyclists to use certain PEDs will allow athletes to legally get ahead in the game without harming their bodies, creating less of a gap between people who use banned substances and people who do not. Critics of Savulescu's plan say that athletes will simply find new ways to get around the rules and that approving drug use sets a poor example for young athletes.

I was always kind of skinny, and thought that I could go on a small cycle and get a bit bigger, and be more attractive to women. I bought some pink pills from a guy at my gym. I think they were called "Diana-ball" [Dianabol]. I thought that was great, because I was trying to meet more girls, and "Diana" is a girl's name ... Before I knew it, my hairline started getting higher and the hair on the back of my head started getting thinner. I was going bald in my early 20s! I stopped using the little pink pills, but it didn't matter. The hair never really grew back, even after I stopped.[36]

Like many steroid users, this young man thought of just the end results he wanted without ever considering the possible side effects from taking the steroids.

Chapter Three

UNDERSTANDING RISK VERSUS REWARD

One key to understanding the widespread use of steroids involves what individuals perceive to be the reward versus the actual risk. Athletes who are under a great deal of pressure from sports organizations, coaches, and fans to push themselves to reach goals that were previously considered unattainable have taken steroids to achieve what they consider to be success. As more and more athletes who have amassed championship victories and shattered records are found to have been using steroids and other PEDs at the time of their achievements, a dangerous example is set for their fellow athletes and especially for younger generations with aspirations of a career in professional sports. Knowing the dangerous, long-term effects from the use of steroids and other PEDs, why do athletes continue doping?

Pro Athletes

The most common instances of steroid abuse are found among professional athletes, even though most professional sports organizations have adopted strict rules against performance-enhancing drug use. Estimates for the number of professional athletes who use steroids vary widely. An anonymous ESPN poll of 143 MLB players in 2014 estimated that 9.4 percent of players were using PEDs, regardless of the strict regulations against them.

MLB officials deny that many players are still using steroids. Rob Manfred, MLB vice president, stated that the drug tests available to the MLB are the most up-to-date, implying that anyone who was taking illegal drugs would be

Part of the pressure to use steroids in baseball comes from the athletes' desire to break records such as the one set by Pete Rose in 1985.

caught. However, Victor Conte, the founder of BALCO, said the tests are not the issue. "What these guys are doing is using fast-acting testosterone, creams, gels, patches and micro-dose injections ... They put this stuff on after a game, let it circulate in their bloodstream, and eight hours later, it's out of their system when they take a drug test. It's so simple."[37] In other words, the fact that very few people fail drug tests does not necessarily mean that very few players take drugs.

According to Canseco, in the past, baseball team owners and other high-ranking club officials were responsible for the surge in steroid use among their players because those in charge of the players' union "fought for years to make sure players wouldn't be tested for steroids." In addition, he said, club owners quietly "put the word out that they want home runs and excitement ... that whatever it is the players are doing to become superhuman, they sure ought to keep it up." Canseco argued that the public agrees with the owners. "People want to be entertained at the ballpark. They want baseball to be fun and exciting. Home runs are fun and exciting ... Steroid-enhanced athletes hit more home runs."[38] Owners and coaches may or may not still be secretly encouraging players to do what they can to make the game exciting, but players may still feel pressure to live up to fans' expectations.

Athletes and Steroids

Following Canseco's mindset, many athletes—whether in high school, college, the pros, or the Olympics—may begin taking steroids because they want to be the best athlete in their sport. Nathan Jendrick, a personal trainer and former competitor in amateur body building contests, wrote in his book, *Dunks, Doubles, Doping*:

> *Olympic athletes often consider that representing their countries is an honor. Other professional athletes, while not representing their country, represent themselves and want simply to show the world they are the top athlete in their profession. Of course, with that comes big money, endorsement deals for products they don't always use, shoes named after them, and a slew of admirers ... not a bad deal, really.*[39]

It is true that steroids often deliver the desired results for athletes, helping them achieve record-breaking status in their sport. Records set at the Olympics as well as in professional sports such as Major League Baseball and the National Football League that stood for many decades were shattered by athletes who either are suspected of or have been found guilty of steroid use.

Many student athletes fall prey to the mindset that bigger muscles give them an advantage and turn to steroids to achieve a larger size. Dan Nieboer, a football, track, and powerlifting coach at a Texas high school, warned his athletes about trying to bulk up. There are, he said, "muscles that work well for them as an athlete and muscles that look good.

They don't necessarily go hand in hand." Bulging biceps, he continued, are "not necessarily going to make you a better basketball player or football player." Furthermore, he told his student athletes that teen bodies are not meant to have bulging muscles. The bones and muscles in teenage bodies are still developing. "With the faster metabolism at the age of 15 or 16, you're not going to get huge. You will increase and get bigger gradually, but not until you're 22 or 23,"[40] he asserted. In addition, the bodies of teens and youth do not handle steroid use well while they are still developing. Steroids can cause the young body's growth plates to fuse together, stunting a young adult's growth permanently.

The Asterisk

Some sportswriters and baseball fans cheered at the news that an asterisk would be placed beside Hall of Famers who were proven to have taken steroids. They believe that all players who take steroids should have asterisks next to their statistics, since without steroids, they might not have been able to achieve their high records. Unsurprisingly, some players disagree. Barry Bonds said in a 2007 interview, "I don't think you can put an asterisk in the game of baseball, and I don't think the Hall of Fame can accept an asterisk ... You cannot give people the freedom, the right to alter history."[41] Although Bonds has not yet been elected to the Hall of Fame, the organization did display the ball he hit to break Hank Aaron's record. The ball is marked with an asterisk, which prompted Bonds to declare that he would boycott the Hall of Fame even if he were inducted.

Not everyone believes athletes who take steroids have tainted sports records, however. Years ago, Canseco asserted that steroids were good for the game of baseball. He predicted that someday, "every baseball player and pro athlete will be using at least low levels of steroids. As a result, baseball and other sports will be more exciting and entertaining."[42] Many fans seemed to agree with Canseco at first. While Canseco, Bonds, and Alex Rodriguez all were heckled by fans in the

The ball Barry Bonds hit to break Hank Aaron's home run record has since been marked with an asterisk, denoting that Bonds's record is tarnished by steroid use.

stands for using steroids, sportswriter Michael Wilbon said in 2004 that he saw few signs of outrage from fans about steroid use. Most fans who responded to his news stories and columns on steroid use by athletes seemed indifferent, he wrote. "For every e-mail expressing true outrage ... there are five from fans who either still don't know exactly what to feel or are more hurt or annoyed than angry."[43] However, a 2016 study found that the memorabilia of players who used steroids declined in value by up to 90 percent. No other behavior affected auction prices as much, according to the *New York Post*:

> *Lance Armstrong ... was found to be "the biggest loser" of the athletes studied, with a decline in memorabilia value of 90 percent from 2013 levels ... Baseball stars Alex Rodriguez, Barry Bonds and Mark McGwire ... saw an 80 percent decline in collectible value from their respective peak careers ... In contrast, memorabilia belonging to [Tiger] Woods and [O. J.] Simpson has declined in value from their career peaks by only 45 percent and 50 percent, respectively.*[44]

Woods was condemned by the press for cheating on his wife multiple times, while Simpson was put on trial for the murder of his ex-wife. This study shows that some fans disapprove more of unethical actions that affect the game than ones that only affect the players' personal lives.

What Is Fair?

Athletes who admit to using steroids say they do so because they want the bigger muscles, the extra strength, the greater endurance, and the faster recovery time after working out that steroids give them. Ken Caminiti, one of the first Major League Baseball players to admit to using steroids, said that athletes who use steroids do not consider the drug use to be cheating because the drugs simply allow them to live up to their potential. Baseball, he said, is "still a hand-eye coordination game, but the difference [with

Athletes who take steroids are often trying to build muscle so they can become stronger.

steroids] is the ball is going to go a little farther. Some of the balls that would go to the warning track will go out. That's the difference."[45]

Caminiti and others assert that while steroids may enhance an athlete's natural abilities, such as running, lifting weights, and throwing balls, the athlete still has to have the ability to do these things well in the first place. According to Bonds, using steroids is absolutely immaterial to how well an athlete plays. "In baseball it really doesn't matter what you do; you still have to hit that baseball," he told reporters after hitting a two-run home run. "If you're incapable of hitting it, it doesn't matter what you take. You have to have eye-hand coordination to be able to produce. I think [steroid use] is really irrelevant to the game of baseball."[46]

In addition, these athletes must go through a rigorous training schedule to take advantage of the benefits bestowed by steroids. One of the primary benefits of using steroids is that they build muscles. When athletes work out while taking steroids, the steroids help the muscles become bigger than they would have been otherwise. Athletes also develop greater endurance and speed due to the steroids' muscle-building effects than if they had worked out without using steroids. Another very important aspect of steroid usage is that they help athletes' muscles recover from a workout faster. All these benefits allow an athlete to train harder and for longer periods of time, which results in greater gains in strength, endurance, and speed than would otherwise be possible. Perhaps most importantly, these key benefits disappear if the athlete stops taking steroids or working out. According to Alva Noë, a philosophy professor at the University of California–Berkeley:

> *Discipline, determination, drive, a willingness to put in the hard hours of training and studying the game—those are the fruits of human labor, and we credit players for rising to the challenge. I think part of what offends the sports fan is the idea that steroids and human growth hormone are a substitute for hard work ... You'd have to be crazy to think steroids or other performance-enhancing drugs are a substitute for hard work. As with any worthwhile bit of human technology, steroids are effective only if used correctly; they work only in a context; indeed, they work only in the context of the training regimen of the athlete.*[47]

What Caminiti, Bonds, Noë, and others contend is that the athlete must have the natural ability to be a great athlete. Taking steroids will not transform someone who has never played a sport before into a superstar.

Is It "Natural"?

Those who believe that steroids and amphetamine are just another training aid argue that taking a performance-enhancing substance is no different from any other method of improving natural ability. These athletes believe that if athletes are allowed to use surgery or high-altitude training to enhance their skills, then athletes should also be permitted to use pharmaceutical aids such as steroids. All three of these common practices give athletes a competitive edge. Tiger Woods underwent LASIK eye surgery to improve his vision to 20/15, which means he can see at a distance of 20 feet (6 m) what most people can see at 15 feet (4.6 m). The surgery was not much of a change for Woods, who was already wearing contact lenses that gave him 20/15 vision. Being able to see the lay of the land more clearly in golf, or the trajectory of a pitch in baseball, would give the athlete an advantage over other players whose vision is not as good. Sportswriter Randy Cohen asked rhetorically, "If laser surgery, why not steroids?"[48]

Cohen also concluded, "We admire athletes who work hard, even risking injury, to improve their play. It is oddly paradoxical to damn those who do just that—albeit pharmaceutically."[49] Another common, and perhaps the most acceptable, enhancement is drinking coffee, tea, or cola for the caffeine to feel more alert.

Some people who are against the use of steroids in sports are not against the use of amphetamine because they feel it is closer to caffeine than to steroids. Actor and sportswriter Brett Ballantini argued that steroids should be banned because they can produce permanent long-term changes in body composition, but amphetamine should not because the changes it causes are temporary. He also believed that the negative side effects such as nausea and dizziness that an amphetamine user might experience would compensate for any boost to concentration and speed.

Others do not agree with Ballantini's views. Rob Neyer, a writer for *SB Nation*, responded to Ballantini by saying that cheating is cheating, whether someone cheats a lot or a little. He argued:

I still cannot see any distinction, integrity-wise, between using amphetamines in 1980 and using steroids in 2000. In both cases, players were using drugs illegally. In both

Some people argue that taking Adderall before a game is no more serious than drinking a cup of coffee for caffeine's energy boost. Others disagree.

cases, players were hoping to become better baseball players. In both cases, players were, wittingly or not, hoping to gain edges over players who were not using those same drugs.

Integrity has little or nothing to do with results. If two students cheat on a test and one gets [a] 92 and one gets a 73, does the C student have less integrity than the A student?[50]

Some question the difference between high-altitude training—a natural form of performance enhancement—and the hormone EPO, both of which stimulate the production of red blood cells and help improve an athlete's endurance and stamina. Many endurance athletes train at high altitudes, where oxygen levels in the air are extremely low. High-altitude training stimulates the production of oxygen-carrying red blood cells; when the athletes come back down to lower elevations, their blood still has higher levels of red blood cells, which improves their endurance. Jacob Sullum, author of *Saying Yes: In Defense of Drug Use*, is not sure that these methods of enhancing ability are any more ethical or have any more integrity than using steroids. "Everybody ought to be able to use the same tools. But I don't see what is different in principle between steroids and anything else artificial we do to change our abilities, be it working out, diet, [or] the various medicines people take to recover from injuries."[51]

The Race to Success

When athletes take performance-enhancing drugs and get that edge that will make them just a fraction of a second faster or a little bit stronger, other athletes may feel they also have to take PEDs just to remain competitive. Thomas H. Murray, former president of the Hastings Center, a bioethics research institute, compared athletes taking performance-enhancing drugs to an arms (weapons) race: "The dynamics of drugs in sport bear more than a superficial resemblance to an arms race: each party drives the other further, lest either be left behind." While some argue that if all athletes were allowed to take steroids and other performance-enhancing substances it would level the playing field, Murray and others contend that such a change would come with a high cost to the athletes. "Athletes, caught in the sport arms race, would be pressed to take more and more drugs, in ever wilder combinations and at increasingly higher doses,"[52] which would be risky to athletes' health, Murray maintains.

Moreover, many athletes want to play clean and not be drugged up with different performance enhancers. These clean athletes are in a no-win situation. If they play clean, they are at a competitive disadvantage. If they take steroids and other PEDs, they risk their health, their career (most sports ban athletes who are caught using steroids), and their

Richard Pound helped found the World Anti-Doping Agency (WADA) to uncover performance-enhancing drug use in the Olympics.

reputations. In addition, because some high-profile athletes use steroids, many people assume that all elite athletes take performance-enhancing substances, thus tarnishing the reputations of those who do not.

Rules Exist for a Reason

Almost all sports organizations, both amateur and professional, ban the use of steroids and other performance-enhancing substances. Athletes who take them are therefore violating the rules of their sport. Richard Pound, a founder of WADA, which tests Olympic athletes for banned substances, says that the rules regulating sports are one of the most important elements of the game. The rules may be arbitrary and artificial, he says (such as the size and weight of equipment), but they are rules that the participants agree to abide by. Those who do not respect the rules, who try to get an unfair advantage over their competitors, are cheaters, he asserts. Pound wrote in his book, *Inside Dope: How Drugs Are the Biggest Threat to Sports, Why You Should Care, and What Can Be Done About Them*: "Cheaters are the sociopaths of sport ... All that matters to them is winning at any cost, and they are willing to cheat or willing to be persuaded to cheat in order to win."[53] According to Pound, they do not care about the promises they made to play clean, and their decision to use steroids and other performance-enhancing substances shows that they do not respect their fellow athletes, either.

Many people contend, however, that the argument against a ban on steroids in sports is a circular argument. They assert that according to the circular argument, steroids are illegal because they are bad, and steroids are bad because they are illegal. The reason for the conclusion is simply a restatement of the conclusion. Along these lines are the arguments that using steroids is immoral and wrong. Joe Lindsey, a contributing writer for *Bicycling* magazine, has written widely about performance-enhancing substances in professional cycling. He writes in an online article, "Doping in sports isn't inherently wrong; it's wrong by the value system with which we judge sports."[54]

Pound responds to this argument by asserting, once again, that "sport cannot exist without rules. And that's the whole point. They are the agreed-upon rules."[55] The rules against doping were developed after many years of studying the issue, he says, and after officials determined that drugs and performance enhancements harm the athletes in physical, psychological, and social ways. Lindsey echoed the conclusions of many when he asked, "Do you want to see who's the best athlete, or just who had the best access to pharmaceutical enhancement?"[56]

Chapter Four

RULES AND REGULATIONS

After understanding the health risks of performance-enhancing drugs and acknowledging the perceived rewards of taking the risk anyway, many athletic and sporting organizations began to structure strict bans on steroids for their athletes. To ensure that success in sports and athletic competition is achieved by way of healthy treatment of the athlete's body and carefully honed natural skill, these organizations set out to use strict consequences to punish anyone found to be using steroids. However, finding new ways to discover, as well as discourage, steroid use has proved a greater challenge than many imagined.

A Ban on Steroids

The problem with banning drugs is that the organization must have some way of backing up the ban. Simply because an organization such as the IOC or MLB says that athletes may not take steroids does not mean the athletes will stop taking performance enhancers. One of the first organizations to ban doping in sporting competitions was the International Association of Athletics Federations, which banned performance enhancements in 1928. However, no method of testing for banned substances had yet been developed, so athletes competed on the honor system. Eventually, by the mid-1960s, a few tests had been developed for detecting drug use, prompting more organizations to prohibit athletes from taking performance-enhancing substances. The governing organizations for soccer and cycling banned doping in 1966. The IOC followed suit the next year and placed

CONSEQUENCES: A COMPARISON

Professional sporting organizations in the United States have set their own rules and policies concerning steroid use. Not only do their policies differ on which drugs are and are not permitted, but the penalties each organization imposes for violations vary widely. Below is a sampling from many major sports organizations.

Organization	1st Violation	2nd Violation	3rd Violation
NFL (16 games in a regular season)	6 games maximum	10 games	2 seasons
NBA (82 games in a regular season)	20 games	45 games	Lifetime ban
NHL (82 games in a regular season)	20 games	60 games	Lifetime ban
MLB (162 games in a regular season)	80 games	1 season	Lifetime ban
Olympics	2 years	Lifetime ban	

steroids on its list of banned substances in 1975. Testing for steroids became much more common in later years after some formerly Communist countries, such as Russia and East Germany, began implementing a secret state-sponsored doping program in order to win medals at the Olympics. Sensing that the athletes' sudden and amazing results were due to performance-enhancing drugs, IOC officials were determined to develop drug tests that could prove the athletes were taking steroids and therefore cheating.

Thomas Bach is the president of the International Olympic Committee. The organization has banned steroid use in the Olympic Games.

Olympic Gold Revoked

One of the most notorious early doping scandals in the sports world centered on Canadian sprinter Ben Johnson at the Summer Olympic Games in Seoul, South Korea, in 1988. In the early 1980s, Johnson had lost many important 100-meter races to American sprinter Carl Lewis. In 1985, Johnson started winning his races against Lewis and setting world records by just hundredths of a second. Johnson beat Lewis at the World Championships in Rome in 1987 by one-tenth of a second, setting a new world record. After this loss, Lewis said, without naming names, that he, too, could win if he were taking drugs. The rivalry between the two sprinters made their matchup at the Olympics a highly anticipated event. Johnson ran the 100-meter race in another world-record time of 9.79 seconds for the gold medal; Lewis, with a time of 9.92 seconds—an American record—had to settle for second place. However, three days later it was revealed that Johnson had tested positive for steroids, and he was stripped of his gold medal, which was then given to Lewis. Johnson later admitted he had been using steroids at the time of the 1987 World Championship race, and he was stripped of that win as well.

After this scandal, Congress passed the Anti-Drug Abuse Act of 1988 that changed the penalty for possessing or distributing steroids without a prescription from a misdemeanor to a felony. All 50 states had already passed laws controlling all aspects of anabolic steroid use, including manufacturing, distributing, possessing, and prescribing. Then, in 1990, Congress passed the Anabolic Steroid Control Act that made steroids a Schedule III drug. (Schedule III drugs are drugs that have a medical purpose and have a low to moderate potential for abuse or addiction.) The categorization of steroids as a Schedule III drug made it a federal crime to use, possess, sell, or dispense steroids without a prescription.

The Opposition

The conversion of steroids from simply a prescription medicine to a controlled substance with all kinds of regulations governing its

STUDENTS USE PEDS, TOO

Seeing professional athletes use performance-enhancing drugs has encouraged some high school and college athletes to do the same. The ease of buying drugs on the Internet means that steroids, HGH, and Adderall are more widely available than ever, and some athletes may take them to gain a competitive edge in their sport. However, the danger of steroid use is increased for young adults. Not only can steroids and HGH cause the same negative effects that professional athletes experience, but in young adults who are still going through puberty, they can also "interfere with the natural development of hormones. Especially in teens, steroids can cause bone growth to stop before it is complete—meaning a child may not reach his or her full adult height."[1]

Adderall abuse is also widespread among students. Young adults with ADHD who are prescribed the medication may share it with friends who want to boost their sports or academic performance. When they abuse it, either by crushing and snorting it or taking too many pills at once, they put themselves at greater risk for heart failure and stroke, especially after doing strenuous exercise.

1. Dr. Manny Alvarez, "A Dangerous Trend: Kids and Teens Using Steroids," Fox News, November 19, 2012. www.foxnews.com/health/2012/11/19/dangerous-trend-kids-and-teens-using-steroids.html.

distribution and possession did not go unopposed. The directors of the Drug Enforcement Administration (DEA) and Health and Human Services testified before a Senate Judiciary Committee that anabolic steroids did not meet the requirements to be classified as a Schedule III drug. In addition, the American Medical Association (AMA) opposed making steroids a Schedule III drug

The United States Drug Enforcement Administration classifies steroids as a Schedule III drug. People who use them without a prescription face harsh penalties.

because, according to the association's representative Edward Langston, "abuse of steroids does not lead to the physical or psychological dependence as is required for scheduling."[57] Nevertheless, Congress was persuaded by two arguments to reclassify steroids: Steroids give the athletes who use them an unfair advantage, and athletes who use steroids are sending a message to the nation's youth that it is acceptable to cheat to win.

Making Headlines

Despite the example set by stripping Ben Johnson of his gold medal, athletes continued to take steroids. One sport that is particularly plagued by doping scandals is professional cycling, especially the grueling Tour de France race, which has had allegations of doping nearly every year for two decades. Entire teams have been eliminated due to drug raids and positive drug tests. In 1998, an assistant with a cycling team sponsored by watch manufacturing company Festina was arrested for possession of growth hormone, testosterone, amphetamines, and EPO. Police raided hotels used by Tour de France cyclists and found more steroids and performance-enhancing substances. After arrests and withdrawals from the race, fewer than half the cyclists who started the race crossed the finish line.

Such incidents prompted cycling officials to initiate harsher penalties and stricter drug tests, but people are still suspicious of professional cyclists' integrity. Chris Froome, a British cyclist, was accused of doping when he won the Tour de France in 2013, simply because Lance Armstrong had admitted to doing it in the past. Armstrong claimed it was impossible to win the race without drugs—a claim that other winners' negative drug tests have proven false. In another race a year later, Froome was allowed to compete while using legally prescribed corticosteroids for a medical condition. When he won, Nicole Cook, a former Olympic cycling champion, criticized officials for giving Froome an exemption, stating that it was not fair to the other competitors.

The immense publicity and embarrassment following the Tour de France drug raids encouraged members of the IOC and various sporting organizations to coordinate their anti-doping efforts by creating WADA. WADA is an independent and international drug testing agency supported by the IOC and participating nations. It researches new performance-enhancing substances and methods to detect them, provides education about doping in sports, and develops and monitors a list of substances that have been banned from sports.

Professional cycling has seen more than one serious doping scandal.

Prior to the establishment of WADA, each sporting organization had its own list of banned substances and different penalties for using them. WADA has encouraged most international sporting federations and governing bodies to follow its Anti-Doping Code, which imposes extremely severe penalties on athletes who are caught doping. Athletes who are caught using steroids or other performance-enhancing substances are banned from participating in their sport for two years. A second offense results in a lifetime ban.

Under the WADA Anti-Doping Code, athletes are 100 percent responsible for any banned substance found during drug tests:

> *It is each Athlete's personal duty to ensure that no Prohibited Substance enters his or her body. Athletes are responsible for any Prohibited Substance ... found to be present in their bodily specimens. Accordingly, it is not necessary that intent, fault, negligence, or knowing Use on the Athlete's part be demonstrated in order to establish an anti-doping violation.*[58]

In other words, athletes will still be guilty of a doping violation if they take a "vitamin" pill from their coach or trainer, and the "vitamin" is actually a banned substance, or if they take a substance they did not know was prohibited under the WADA Anti-Doping Code. If banned substances are found during drug tests, the athlete is guilty, no matter how it came to be in the athlete's body.

Drug Testing

Penalties for banned drug use are not nearly as severe in the professional sports leagues in the United States. In fact, actually getting professional athletes to submit to testing is not as easy as it is for the elite athletes such as Olympians, professional cyclists, and track and field athletes. Professional athletes have used their collective bargaining agreements and players' unions to fight mandatory testing, citing concerns for players' privacy. Now, however, the professional sports organizations require athletes to undergo drug testing. Standards have become much stricter in most of the leagues in recent years, although critics say that some of them are still too lenient.

The National Basketball Association (NBA) was one of the first professional sporting organizations to initiate drug testing. At the time the policy was introduced, athletes were tested

An NFL player can fail his drug test if the results detect a drug designed to hide the presence of steroids.

for illegal drugs and performance-enhancing substances only if evidence was uncovered that demonstrated the athlete was using drugs. However, after accusations that it was being too lenient on its players, the NBA instituted a stricter testing program: Each player is randomly selected for testing four times during the season and twice during the offseason. A basketball player who tests positive for steroids must enter a substance abuse program and is suspended for 20 games for a first offense (out of a possible 82 games in a regular season), 45 games for a second offense, and is given a lifetime ban for a third violation.

The National Football League began testing its players in 1987. A computer randomly selects five players from eight teams to be tested during the preseason and regular season. Only teams that have made the playoffs are tested in the postseason. Players cannot be given blood tests more than six times per year, and the tests cannot take place on game days. Players who test positive for steroids or performance-enhancing substances receive a suspension of up to six games, depending on what they test positive for; a ten-game suspension is given for a second violation, and a third positive drug test results in a two-year suspension. In addition, if a drug test result shows the presence of a "masking" agent (a drug typically taken to cover up the presence of an illegal drug or steroid), even if no steroid is detected, the player receives the appropriate suspension as well. Suspensions in football are a little more serious than in basketball, as there are much fewer games in a regular season.

Amphetamine is considered by the NFL to be a recreational drug rather than a performance-enhancing one. It is still banned, but the policy is different: Players are tested only once per year, during the preseason. Currently, the policy in the NFL is to announce a player's failed drug test, but not to identify the type of drug that caused him to fail. This has led to many players announcing that they failed their drug test due to Adderall use. It is uncertain whether this is true or whether they are trying to cover up for failing because they took a drug that has more stigma, or shame, attached to it.

Major League Baseball was one of the last sporting organizations to crack down on its players who use performance-enhancing drugs. The organization banned steroids in 1991, but the players were not tested and the ban was largely ignored. A sports reporter wrote about seeing the steroid androstenedione in Mark McGwire's locker in 1998, but MLB did not punish him for it. Finally in 2003, baseball players were submitted to drug testing that determined that 5 to 7 percent of baseball players used steroids and other performance-enhancing substances (although some insiders say the percentage of steroid users is much higher). The drug test results were supposed to

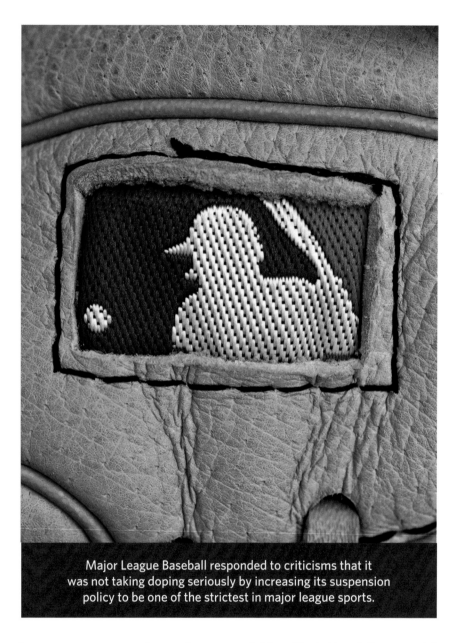

Major League Baseball responded to criticisms that it was not taking doping seriously by increasing its suspension policy to be one of the strictest in major league sports.

be anonymous, and no player would be disciplined for steroid use; the tests were considered to be a survey to see how widespread PED use was within the league. That confidentiality was breached in 2009, though, when *Sports Illustrated* magazine revealed that Alex Rodriguez had tested positive for steroids in the anonymous survey.

Until 2004, baseball players who tested positive did not face any kind of penalty for using a banned substance. That year, players who did test positive for steroids and other banned drugs were sent to a counselor. The following year, the policy was changed again to a 10-game suspension for first-time users, and 12 players were suspended for testing positive for steroids. After the 2005 season ended, the suspensions were changed again, this time to 50 games for first-time users, and since then, 56 more players have been suspended. In 2014, after the Biogenesis scandal broke, the penalties were increased even further, to 80 games for first-time users. Additionally, "under the new rules, any player testing positive for banned drugs will face six unannounced urine tests and three blood tests during every year of his remaining career."[59] Baseball has gone from having one of the lightest suspension policies to one of the strictest, since there are 162 games in a regular season. A player who is suspended for 80 games is out for half the season. In addition to increasing this penalty, the league closed several loopholes that allowed players to profit even if they had been suspended. If a player's team makes the MLB playoffs, they will play more games that year, which meant that a player who was suspended for 162 games could still collect a partial salary. The new regulations ensured that players who are suspended for a season will lose their entire year's salary, rather than being able to collect for those extra games. They are also ineligible for the postseason. Many people feel that these new rules show the league is finally serious about eliminating steroid use from the game.

Drug Testing in Educational Sports

Professional and elite-level athletes are not the only athletes who are tested for performance-enhancing drugs. Testing for steroids has spread to colleges and high schools as well. The percentage of athletes who use steroids at the college and high school level has more than doubled in recent years, according to a study released by the Partnership for Drug-Free Kids. The study found that in

"I HAVE NEVER TESTED POSITIVE"

Marion Jones, who won three gold and two bronze medals in track at the 2000 Olympics in Sydney, was implicated in the BALCO steroid scandal by Victor Conte, the owner of the Bay Area Laboratory Co-Operative. Through an anonymous tip, Conte was discovered to be selling an undetectable steroid to his clients, who included Marion Jones, Barry Bonds, and Bill Romanowski, among others. Jones denied the allegations of steroid use to the press and to a grand jury investigating the BALCO scandal, saying:

My response all along is the fact I've never accepted nor taken nor been offered any performance-enhancing drug from anyone ... That's the truth. That's what I'm going to stick with ... My life does not revolve around having to prove to anyone that I am drug free. I am probably one of the most tested athletes in the world. I have never tested positive for a steroid. The people that know me ... know I would never do anything illegal. I would never take any performance-enhancing drug. I'm not going to degrade myself to prove I'm drug free. I know I am.[1]

Jones was convicted in 2007 of lying to the grand jury and was sentenced to six months in jail. She was also stripped of her wins and medal from the 2000 Olympics.

2013, 11 percent of high school students reported illegally using HGH at least once in their lifetime, compared to only 5 percent the previous year.

Illinois and New Jersey are the only states that require high school athletes be tested for steroids. Texas used to test for steroids, beginning in February 2008. By the end of the fall 2008

Track star Marion Jones was stripped of her Olympic titles after it was discovered that she had used steroids to win them.

1. Quoted in John Crumpacker, "Marion Jones Isn't Running from Steroid Controversy," *San Francisco Chronicle*, May 14, 2004. www.sfgate.com/cgi-bin/article.cgi% 3Ff%3D/chronicle/archive/2004/05/14/SPGN86L3NH1.DTL.

semester, nearly 29,000 student athletes had been tested. Only 11 high school athletes tested positive for steroids. In 2015, the testing law in Texas was repealed. Similarly, Florida suspended

A LIE, MASQUERADING AS THE TRUTH

Many athletes who are accused of taking steroids often respond to the accusation by saying "I have never tested positive." Richard Pound, a founder of WADA, explained why people should not take this response as proof that the athlete is "clean" and has never doped:

"I have never tested positive" has become so common-place that it is a wonder anyone was ever fooled by it. This statement is trotted out as proof that the athletes in question have not doped—no positive result means no doping. End of any possible controversy, they say. But, the statement is true only as far as its contents take it. The only thing it proves is exactly what it says—that the person has never tested positive. It doesn't prove whether or not the person has used the prohibited substances or methods. It simply means that they never got caught if they were doping. Often, it was because there was no test at the time for the substance they were using.[1]

1. Richard Pound, *Inside Dope: How Drugs Are the Biggest Threat to Sports, Why You Should Care, and What Can Be Done About Them.* Mississauga, ON: Wiley, 2006, pp. 84–85.

its steroid testing program after one year because there was only one positive result out of 600 students tested. An Associated Press survey of steroid tests in Illinois, New Jersey, Texas, and Florida found that only 18 tests out of 30,799 came back positive. School administrators and state legislators in the four states initially called the testing program a great success, claiming the tests work as a deterrent to steroid use. State representative Dan Flynn, who sponsored the Texas legislation that authorized the testing, said at the time, "This means that the program is working because the kids know they are being tested and stayed away from steroids."[60]

Critics of testing high school athletes assert, however, that the tests are a waste of money. Matt Bartle, a state senator from Missouri, tried to convince his colleagues to pass a steroid testing program for high school athletes, but when he saw Florida's results, he abandoned the proposal, asking, "Is there enough steroid use out there that spending a couple million bucks a year against everything else that the state needs to spend money on is worth it?"[61] Texas spent $6 million to test 50,000 students over 2 years. Critics say the low number of positive results do not justify the expense.

Moreover, in a study of 197 college student athletes who all volunteered to undergo testing for steroid use, and who all claimed to be clean, two athletes tested positive for steroids. The study's authors, Russell Meldrum and Judy Feinberg, assert that this result shows that testing is not a deterrent to drug use. Despite receiving education on the dangers of steroid use, Meldrum and Feinberg argue, "the decision to not use drugs is felt to be related more to the fear of reprisal [punishment] than to health issues." Moreover, they assert, "the use of anabolic steroids among athletes, although not increasing, has not diminished under the current testing programs."[62]

A Positive Peer Pressure Program

Experts on steroid use agree that the best way to prevent or deter steroid use is through peer pressure. Testing is not "a quick fix," said Linn Goldberg, a doctor who specializes in sports medicine. "There has to be peer pressure to do the right thing."[63] Teens who go through drug education programs together often exert peer pressure on each other to stay clean. Two proven programs are ATLAS and ATHENA, offered by the Oregon Health and Science University. ATLAS is geared toward male athletes, while ATHENA is for females. The university trains the coaches in the principles of the program, but the student athletes are the program's true leaders. The program offers the athletes information on sports nutrition and strength-training exercises. In addition, the student leaders work with their fellow students on role-playing ways to refuse steroids and other drugs, creating campaigns or public service announcements, playing interactive games, and setting goals. The National Institute on Drug Abuse, a government organization that studies drug abuse and addiction, studied more than 3,200 students who had gone through ATLAS and ATHENA a year earlier and found that steroid use among those who had gone through the programs had declined by more than 50 percent. The students said they learned how to stand up for themselves and say no to using steroids. According to Goldberg, the approach used by these programs "exerts positive peer pressure and promotes positive role modeling."[64]

Chapter Five

WHAT CAN BE DONE IN THE FUTURE?

Enforcing new rules for steroid use in sports is a complex issue for sporting organizations. Part of that issue is that the testing of blood, urine, and hair samples is always trying to catch up to the new advancements of the drug market. As new synthetic steroids are designed, the scope of steroid testing falls behind, and sports organizations race to keep up with the market for new drugs that fly under the radar but still enhance performance.

Norethandrolone

One of the greatest scandals involving steroids in sports illustrates how difficult it is to keep up with the development of new performance-enhancing drugs. In the summer of 2002, a routine urine sample from cyclist Tammy Thomas was sent for testing to a drug analysis laboratory called the Olympic Analytical Laboratory at the University of California–Los Angeles. At first glance, the sample showed no signs of steroids or banned substances, but did appear off. A second test showed the presence of a steroid known as norethandrolone. The scientists were surprised at the presence of this drug, since it had originally been patented by Wyeth Pharmaceuticals during the 1960s before falling into obscurity, without ever being commercially manufactured.

According to Don H. Catlin, director of the Olympic Analytical Laboratory, there were two possible scenarios for the reemergence of this steroid. "One," he said, "there was a scientist from Wyeth who had squirreled away a supply" and had kept quiet on its existence for decades, a possibility he felt did not make much sense. The alternative, he said, was that "there was a rogue scientist out there making it."[65] After discovering that the steroid could easily be made by someone who had the right equipment and ingredients, Catlin realized that science would be continually trying to detect new and previously undetectable versions of banned performance-enhancing substances. The steroid business had suddenly become very sophisticated.

The Bay Area Laboratory Co-Operative

The following summer, Trevor Graham, a well-known track coach at the time, called USADA to say he knew several high-profile track stars who were using undetectable performance-enhancing drugs. He sent a syringe with some residue in the needle to the USADA office, which in turn sent it to Catlin's laboratory in Los Angeles for identification. Catlin assured Rich Wanninger at USADA that the substance was probably harmless; his lab received unknown materials all the time that generally turned out to be nothing. Wanninger, however, was convinced that it was a new drug, and with the U.S. Track and Field championships just a few days away, he wanted an immediate answer as to whether it was a performance-enhancing drug so that the athletes could be tested for it.

Catlin soon discovered that the substance was indeed a new and previously undetectable steroid. The steroid was closely related to two other known steroids, but its molecular structure had been deliberately altered to avoid detection during standard drug tests. Catlin named the designer steroid tetrahydrogestrinone, or THG, and created a test to detect it. The new drug test was created just in time for the track and field championships. Catlin's lab secretly tested samples from athletes who competed at the championships and found four positive results. All of the positive results came from athletes who were national champions in their sport: shot-putter Kevin Toth, hammer-throwers John McEwen and Melissa Price, and middle-distance runner Regina Jacobs.

USADA did not announce the results of the tests yet; it was hoping to test more athletes to discover who was using the steroid before word leaked out about its discovery. The International Association of Athletics Federations immediately collected samples from several prominent international athletes, including Dwain Chambers, a British sprinter, and Kelli White, an American sprinter. These athletes and others who were subsequently discovered to be using THG—baseball players Barry Bonds, Jason Giambi, and Gary Sheffield; Oakland Raiders football players Bill Romanowski, Tyrone Wheatley, and Chris Cooper; and cyclist Tammy Thomas—all bought supplements from the same source: the Bay Area Laboratory Co-Operative (BALCO), a nutritional supplements company based in the San Francisco Bay area, owned by Victor Conte.

Undetectable Steroids Brought to Light

Conte bought THG from a chemist on the East Coast, Patrick Arnold, who created the new steroid in order to avoid detection during routine drug tests. Conte marketed and sold THG as the "Clear" to his athlete clients. The Clear was not actually clear, but a mixture of flaxseed oil and steroids that was caramel in color. Athletes took the Clear by placing a few drops of the liquid under the tongue. It was called the Clear because athletes who used it were cleared during their drug tests.

Conte sold another steroid he called the "Cream." The Cream contained testosterone and epitestosterone ("epi") in a lotion that was rubbed on the athlete's skin. The Cream was used to mask the presence of steroids taken by the athlete. Steroids suppress the body's natural production of testosterone. One way to detect the presence of steroids in an athlete's body is to test for the presence of testosterone and epitestosterone. Epi is another naturally-occurring substance in the body, although scientists do not know its exact function. Epi and testosterone occur in a one-to-one ratio. However, in athletes who take steroids, the

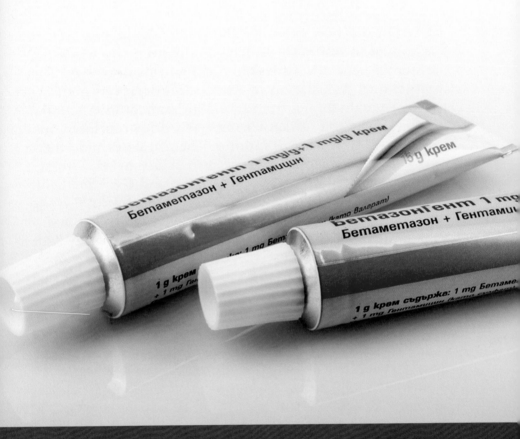

BALCO sold athletes a lotion called the Cream that helped them pass drug tests by hiding the presence of illegal steroids in the body.

epi-to-testosterone ratio changes. When the ratio is higher than six to one, or even four to one in some sports, the athlete is considered to be doping. The Cream works to even out the epi-testosterone ratio, thus masking the effect of doping.

Consequences

The Cream and the Clear symbolize the difficulties inherent in catching steroid users. Rogue chemists are continually tinkering with the formulations for steroids, trying to create new drugs and performance-enhancing substances that will evade detection in drug tests. Athletes who are illegally taking steroids can typically pass a drug test by stopping use of the drug several days before the test, but if the test is random and unannounced, they are obviously unable to use this method. This makes undetectable steroids an appealing idea. While steroids are a controlled substance, the penalties for those who create and sell new, undetectable steroids have often been light. Arnold was sentenced to three months in prison and three months of home confinement for creating the Clear; Conte, who sold it, received a four-month prison sentence.

The penalties for athletes who use steroids in amateur or elite-level sports are much harsher, on the other hand. For athletes who compete in the Olympics and their sport's national championships, getting caught using steroids means an automatic two-year suspension. A second offense will ban them for life. Some have been stripped of their medals after being caught. Professional athletes, for the most part, do not face such strict penalties for steroid use, although most professional sports are increasing their penalties. Most professional sports suspend an athlete without pay for a specified number of games, with each subsequent violation earning a higher number of games suspended.

Penalties for using, importing, or selling illegal drugs are much harsher than the bans sports leagues institute. These punishments can include high fines and jail time. In 2016, Nick Brandt-Sorenson, a former professional cyclist, sold EPO that he had imported from another country. Importing illegal drugs is a federal offense. As punishment, Brandt-Sorenson was fined $5,000, ordered to complete 300 hours of community service, and sentenced to 3 years of probation instead of jail time.

Many professional athletes believe it is worth the risk to take "undetectable" steroids. Those who use these new designer steroids get all the benefits of using steroids—increased muscle mass, increased strength, faster recovery from workouts—with little worry of getting caught by drug tests.

Romanowski, the former Oakland Raiders football player who was caught using the Clear during the BALCO scandal, said he "took considerable pride in trying to outsmart the system ... I was taking performance-enhancing substances they couldn't test for, like THG. As soon as I found out something could be tested for, I stopped taking it."[66]

A *Washington Post* study found that it is extremely easy to find new steroids that are currently undetectable in drug tests. The newspaper bought five nutritional supplements online that were advertised to build muscles fast. It then asked Catlin's drug testing lab at the University of California–Los Angeles to analyze the supplements. Catlin found that four of the five supplements were previously unknown steroids. Catlin's laboratory was aware of the fifth steroid, but researchers did not know it was available for purchase by the general public. One official with a nutritional supplement company said it was easy to fool drug testers. "There's an unlimited pool of steroids," he said. "You could do this for the next 100 years ... The longer they don't pay attention the [more rampant] it gets."[67] Moreover, officials with both drug testing labs and supplement companies agree that the light sentences imposed in the BALCO scandal embolden others to get into the field of selling steroids as nutritional supplements.

Furthermore, even the drug testers acknowledge that testing for steroids is a never-ending game of catch-up. Nathan Jendrick, author of *Dunks, Doubles, Doping*, wrote, "As soon as the drug testers catch on to one drug, there will likely be another that is undetectable."[68] It is, he wrote, a "cat and mouse game of cheaters trying to stay ahead of the drug testers" which is "a recipe for disaster."[69] Because they are constantly altering and tweaking the composition of steroids to come up with new designer steroids, the creators do not know what effects these changes will have on the human body when they are ingested.

In 2014, *Bleacher Report* wrote about a new, undetectable drug called mechano growth factor (MGF) that was rumored to be available at the 2014 Winter Olympics at Sochi. USADA had been aware of its availability since 2008 but had not done anything to stop its sale. No further stories about MGF use were reported, but it is unclear whether or not athletes are using it because there is no reliable test for it yet.

Rewards over Penalties

Since it is not yet possible for drug testers to design a test to detect steroids that do not exist yet, or that are not known to exist, some people believe there must be other ways to end doping in sports. Catlin, who has been testing athletes for illegal substances since 1984, believes there must be a better way. "Science can't solve all the problems," he said. "For me—who ... believed we could do it just with doping control and testing—to say it's not working is a bit of a change."[70] Catlin experimented with an idea that rewards athletes for staying clean instead of punishing them for doping.

His Volunteer Program would have made athletes prove that they were clean, rather than having scientists prove they were doping. In his program, athletes would be tested frequently. Their test results would form a baseline biological profile. Any spike in the athlete's levels of testosterone, hemoglobin, or other body chemistry levels would indicate drug use, even if traditional drug tests showed no indication of any banned substances.

While Catlin's Volunteer Program never got off the ground, a similar program, Project Believe, run by USADA, was in place in time for the 2008 Summer Olympics in Beijing. Twelve athletes participated in the program, including decathlete Bryan Clay and swimmers Michael Phelps and Dara Torres. Torres, a 41-year-old swimmer who had already won gold medals in 4 previous Olympics, faced enormous scrutiny over her decision to return to racing. Many were suspicious that her record-breaking qualifying times were due to her use of illegal substances.

Open to Testing

To prove that she was clean, Torres went to the USADA headquarters to meet with Travis Tygart, the agency's chief executive officer, and demand that she be tested. Tygart said he was skeptical when Torres appeared in his office asserting she was clean. He remembered that Marion Jones, an American track star who also had insisted she was clean, had had no indications of banned substances show up in her drug test results, but then was forced to admit during the BALCO scandal that she had used undetectable steroids obtained from BALCO. "You're telling us all the same stuff Marion told us when we met with her and you're saying all the right things,"[71] Tygart told Torres. "Why should I believe you?"[72] Torres responded by saying USADA could test her at any time and could use hair, urine, blood, or DNA so she could prove she was not using banned substances. "I decided to become an open book, and asked to be tested in any way they want to show I'm clean," she said. "I understand if I just sat there and said I passed my tests, that people wouldn't believe me. I've gone beyond the call of duty to prove I'm clean, but you are guilty until proven innocent in this day and age, so what else can I do?"[73]

Tygart then told Torres about USADA's new program, Project Believe. While participating in the program, Torres provided urine and blood samples every couple of weeks, which tested her biological markers looking for signs of performance-enhancing substances. Although the results showed no signs that Torres had been using any kind of banned substances, USADA cannot guarantee she was not doping. "The science is not at the stage where we can give a 100 percent guarantee to any athlete that they are clean," Tygart said. "But if they aren't clean, then they would have to be a fool, or a huge risk taker to do a program like this."[74]

Currently, USADA uses the Athlete Biological Passport (ABP) in its fight against doping. The ABP, like Project Believe, monitors an athlete's blood and urine over time. It is only one of the ways USADA fights drug use in sports.

The Landscape of Sports and Steroids

Steroids cause both long-term and short-term negative effects on the body, but athletes continue to use them to reach new goals for athletic excellence. New drugs are developed faster than the testing technology can keep up, and a vicious cycle is created. What is needed, according to Shaun Assael, author of *Steroid Nation*, is a culture change in how Americans view athletes who are caught doping. In addition, athletes must change the way they think about steroids and amphetamines, a requirement that will not be easy.

When a reporter wrote about discovering androstenedione in Mark McGwire's locker in 1998, both baseball fans and the well-respected *New York Times* did not think that his use of what was then a legal nutritional supplement (but is now classified as a steroid) occurred under "questionable circumstances."[75] The prevailing attitude of both the public and the media, according to John Hoberman of the University of Texas–Austin, "was that the use of 'Andro' was (a) a private matter and (b) irrelevant to the integrity of the game." Hoberman argued that the media coverage of McGwire's use of a disputed performance-enhancing substance "was only the latest evidence of our society's basically tolerant attitude toward doping"[76] in sports. He concluded that the public is more interested in sporting success stories than in sporting contests that are free of drugs.

In more recent years, athletes such as Alex Rodriguez and Lance Armstrong have become outcasts in their sports and among fans, as their long-term, adamant denial of using performance-enhancing drugs followed by an eventual admittance of guilt caused both distrust and disgust. Not only do the fans feel betrayed, but the organizations, teams, and sponsors feel they cannot depend on the athletes and an attempt has been made to distance themselves.

In the case of Rodriguez, he returned to play for the New York Yankees in 2015 after serving his 162-game suspension, but the response from both the fans and the Yankee clubhouse was never the same. In August 2016, after

Mark McGwire's steroid scandal occurred during a time when the public's view of sports was that an athlete's record was more important than what he or she might be doing to achieve it.

spending weeks on the bench, Rodriguez announced he would be playing his last game for the New York Yankees and taking an advisor position with the team, away from the spotlight.

In Lance Armstrong's case, he gave an interview to BBC Sport in 2015, stating that, while he would not likely have made the same choices if he were racing today, if he could be transported back to the mid-nineties "when it was completely and totally pervasive, I would probably do it again."[77] Armstrong is currently banned from competitive cycling for life.

However, even with all of these negative consequences, athletes continue to take performance-enhancing drugs for fear they will not be able to keep up with the other athletes in their field. The temptation of winning awards, fame, and money is sometimes too much for athletes and coaches to resist. In 2014, Russia was the focus of a scandal when it was discovered that the government had sponsored a doping program for its athletes. As a result, more than 300 athletes were not allowed to compete in the 2016 Rio Summer Games.

According to Sanjay Gupta, a medical correspondent for several media outlets, athletes will not change their behavior concerning performance-enhancing drugs until society changes its views about athletes who dope. Gupta explained: "You as the athlete have in your mind how you want to be remembered. That's why you put yourself through such excruciating pain day in and day out to get there. And if that legacy is on the line, if the political winds turn, and suddenly anybody associated with these things are looked at as bad people, in an era of cheating, that's the deterrent."[78]

The greatest power that exists to deter athletes from using steroids is a combination of strict and severe regulations from athletic organizations coupled with support from fans, sponsors, and the media of the natural ability of the athlete. Instead of rewarding doping athletes with massive endorsement deals and a welcome back to their sport after one failed drug test, the public should reward athletes who steer clear of these drugs and push their bodies through conditioning and nutrition to achieve their goals.

Notes

Introduction: An Organization's Epidemic

1. Rafael Palmeiro, Testimony Before the House Committee on Government Reform, March 17, 2005. oversight.house.gov/features/steroids/testimony_palmeiro.PDF.

2. Quoted in Selena Roberts and David Epstein, "Confronting A-Rod," *Sports Illustrated*, February 16, 2009, p. 28.

3. Quoted in Peter Gammons, "Rodriguez: Sorry and Deeply Regretful," ESPN, February 9, 2009. sports.espn.go.com/mlb/news/story?id=3895281.

4. ESPN.com news services, "A-Rod Confessed in DEA Meeting" ESPN.com, November 6, 2014. www.espn.com/new-york/mlb/story/_/id/11825652/alex-rodriguez-new-york-yankees-admitted-dea-used-peds.

5. Jose Canseco, *Vindicated: Big Names, Big Liars, and the Battle to Save Baseball.* New York, NY: Simon Spotlight Entertainment, 2008, p. 148.

6. Jose Canseco, *Juiced: Wild Times, Rampant 'Roids, Smash Hits, and How Baseball Got Big.* New York, NY: Regan, 2005, p. 170.

7. Canseco, *Vindicated*, p. 148.

8. George J. Mitchell, *Report to the Commissioner of Baseball of an Independent Investigation into the Illegal Use of Steroids and Other Performance-Enhancing Substances by Players in Major League Baseball*, Office of the Commissioner of Baseball, December 13, 2007, p. SR-8. files.mlb.com/mitchrpt.pdf.

9. Jesse Haggard, *Demystifying Steroids*. Bloomington, IN: AuthorHouse, 2008, p. 14.

10. Daniel Sundfeld Spiga Real et al., "Oxandrolone Use in Adult Burn Patients: Systematic Review and Meta-analysis," *Acta Cirurgica Brasileira*, vol. 29, supl. 3, 2014. www.scielo.br/scielo.php?script=sci_arttext&pid=S0102-86502014001500068.

11. Quoted in John McCloskey and Julian Bailes, *When Winning Costs Too Much: Steroids, Supplements, and Scandal in Today's Sports*. Lanham, MD: Taylor Trade, 2005, p. 8.

12. Terry Todd, "The Steroid Predicament," *Sports Illustrated*, August 1, 1983. vault.sportsillustrated.cnn.com/vault/article/magazine/MAG1121081/3/index.htm.

13. Richard Pound, *Inside Dope: How Drugs Are the Biggest Threat to Sports, Why You Should Care, and What Can Be Done About Them*. Mississauga, ON: Wiley, 2006, p. 54.

14. Quoted in Michael Janofsky, "Coaches Concede That Steroids Fueled East Germany's Success in Swimming," *New York Times*, December 3, 1991, p. B15.

15. Quoted in Merrell Noden, "A Dirty Coach Comes Clean," *Sports Illustrated*, March 13, 1989, p. 22.

16. Quoted in Mike Fainaru-Wada, "Steroids' Powerful, Troubling Attraction," *San Francisco Chronicle*, July 8, 2004, p. B1.

17. Quoted in Fainaru-Wada, "Steroids' Powerful, Troubling Attraction," p. B1.

18. Quoted in Fainaru-Wada, "Steroids' Powerful, Troubling Attraction," p. B1.

19. Quoted in Brent Schrotenboer, "Players of Substance," *San Diego Union-Tribune*, September 21, 2008. www.signonsandiego.com/union-trib/20080921/news_1s21nflmai.html.

20. Schrotenboer, "Players of Substance."

21. Quoted in Schrotenboer, "Players of Substance."

22. Quoted in Jim Hoagland, "Summer of Skepticism," *Washington Post*, July 29, 2007, B7.

23. Quoted in Tom Verducci, "Totally Juiced," *Sports Illustrated*, June 3, 2002, p. 34.

24. Jose Canseco, *Juiced*, p. 237.

Chapter 2: Effects on the Body

25. Quoted in Wayne Coffey, "Teens' Big Worry: For High School Athletes, Steroids Still the Rage,"

New York Daily News, December 16, 2007. www.nydailynews.com/sports/high_school /2007/12/16/2007-12-16_teens_big_worry_ for_high_school _athletes.html.

26. Dan Clark, *Gladiator: A True Story of 'Roids, Rage, and Redemption*. New York, NY: Scribner, 2009, pp. 32–33.

27. Clark, *Gladiator*, p. 5.

28. Omudhome Ogbru, "Common Side Effects of Adderall," RxList, April 2, 2015. www.rxlist.com/ adderall-side-effects-drug-center.htm.

29. Quoted in Kirsten Sparre, "Doping Harms the Children of Athletes," *Play the Game*, 2008, p. 3.

30. Giselher Spitzer and Sabra Lane, "Doped East German Athletes and Children Suffer Health Problems: Study," ABC Online, November 1, 2007. www.abc.net.au/am/content/2007/ s2078111. htm.

31. Quoted in Tracy Wheeler, "Steroid Expert Says Teens Following Heroes' Lead," *Akron (OH) Beacon Journal*, March 8, 2008.

32. Quoted in Jessica Burkhart, "Scary Steroids," *Listen*, January 2008, p. 6.

33. Quoted in Brittany Stahl, "Despite MLB Scandals, Steroid Use Rampant in College Baseball," *NYC Pavement Pieces*, March 26, 2009. journalism.nyu. edu/pubzone/pavement/in/despite-mlb-scan- dals-steroids-rampant-in-college-baseball.

34. Stan Grossfeld, "When Cheers Turn to Depression," *Boston Globe*, February 19, 2008. www.boston.com/sports/schools/articles/2008/02/19/when_cheers_turn_to_depression.
35. Quoted in Grossfeld, "When Cheers Turn to Depression."
36. Anonymous, "True Stories of Steroid Abuse," Association Against Steroid Abuse. www.steroidabuse.com/true-stories-of-steroid-abuse.html.

Chapter 3: Understanding Risk Versus Reward

37. "Conte: Half of MLB Using PEDs," FOX Sports, August 16, 2012. www.foxsports.com/mlb/story/half-of-players-in-baseball-on-steroids-says-balco-boss-victor-conte-081612.
38. Canseco, *Juiced*, p. 9.
39. Nathan Jendrick, *Dunks, Doubles, Doping: How Steroids Are Killing American Athletics*. Guilford, CT: Lyons Press, 2006, p. 26.
40. Quoted in Darla Atlas, "Teens Using Steroids Cheat Themselves and Their Health," *Dallas Morning News*, February 5, 2008. www.dallasnews.com/sharedcontent/dws/fea/lifetravel/stories/DN-nh_steroid_0205liv.ART.State.Edition1.4567494.html.
41. Quoted in Thom Loverro, "LOVERRO: Barry Bonds Returns to Baseball, but the Asterisk Remains," *The Washington Times*, March

18, 2014. www.washingtontimes.com/news/2014/mar/18/barry-bonds-returns-baseball-asterisk-remains/.

42. Canseco, *Juiced*, p. 2.

43. Michael Wilbon, "Tarnished Records Deserve an Asterisk," *Washington Post*, December 4, 2004, p. D10. www.washingtonpost.com/wp-dyn/articles/A33718-2004Dec3.html.

44. Kathleen Burke, "Steroids, Scandals Damage Prices of Sports Memorabilia," *New York Post*, June 04, 2016. nypost.com/2016/06/04/steroids-scandals-damage-prices-of-sports-memorabilia/.

45. Quoted in Verducci, "Totally Juiced," p. 38.

46. Quoted in Fainaru-Wada, "Steroids' Powerful, Troubling Attraction," p. B1.

47. Alva Noë, "A-Rod Isn't a Cheater," Salon, May 1, 2009. www.salon.com/env/feature/2009/05/01/a_rod_steroids.

48. Randy Cohen, "Is Manny Ramirez Really All That Bad?" *New York Times*, May 19, 2009. ethicist.blogs.nytimes.com/2009/05/19/is-manny-ramirez-really-all-that-bad/?apage=2.

49. Cohen, "Is Manny Ramirez Really All That Bad?"

50. Rob Neyer, "Yup. Still Waiting for Distinction Between Greenies and 'Roids," SBNation, December 30, 2013. www.sbnation.com/2013/12/30/5255996/mlb-

baseball-drugs-peds-steroids-amphetamines-greenies-hall-fame.

51. Quoted in Patrick Hruby, "Let the Juicing Begin," ESPN.com: Page 2, March 10, 2006. sports.espn.go.com/espn/page2/story?page=hruby/060310.

52. Quoted in Mary Crowley, ed., *From Birth to Death and Bench to Clinic: The Hastings Center Bioethics Briefing Book for Journalists, Policymakers, and Campaigns.* Garrison, NY: Hastings Center, 2008, p. 156.

53. Pound, *Inside Dope*, p. 12.

54. Joe Lindsey, "Why Legalizing Sports Doping Won't Work," Freakonomics Blog, *New York Times*, July 27, 2007. freakonomics.blogs.nytimes.com/2007/07/27/why-legalizing-sports-doping-wont-work/.

55. Pound, *Inside Dope*, p. 38.

56. Lindsey, "Why Legalizing Sports Doping Won't Work."

Chapter 4: Rules and Regulations

57. Quoted in John Romano and Rick Collins, "Schedule 3—the Hard Way!" RxMuscle, April 16, 2009. www.rxmuscle.com/articles/romanos-rage/212-schedule-three-the-hard-way.html.

58. Quoted in Mark Conrad, *The Business of Sports: A Primer for Journalists.* Mahwah, NJ: Lawrence Erlbaum, 2006, pp. 234–35.

59. Bob Nightengale, "MLB Toughens Drug Agreement Provisions," *USA Today*, March 28, 2014. www.usatoday.com/story/sports/mlb/2014/03/28/mlb-toughens-drug-agreement-provisions/7023401/.

60. Quoted in Enrique Rangel, "HS Athletes Pass Steroids Test," *Lubbock (TX) Avalanche-Journal*, June 19, 2008. www.lubbockonline.com/stories/061908/loc_292671263.shtml.

61. Quoted in Geoff Mulvihill, "Few Caught by Steroid Testing in High School," StandardNet, March 17, 2009. www.standard.net/live/sports/prepinsider/167292.

62. Russell Meldrum and Judy Feinberg, "Drug Use by College Athletes: Is Testing an Effective Deterrent?" *Sport Journal*, Spring 2002. www.thesportjournal.org/article/drug-use-college-athletes-random-testing-effective-deterrent.

63. Quoted in Mulvihill, "Few Caught by Steroid Testing in High School."

64. Linn Goldberg, Testimony Before the U.S. House of Representatives, Committee on Government Reform, April 27, 2005. oversight.house.gov/documents/200504271119 57-63760.pdf.

65. Don Catlin and Peter Aldhouse, "Ending the Influence," *New Scientist*, August 11, 2007, p. 45.

66. Bill Romanowski and Adam Shefter, *Romo*. New York, NY: HarperCollins, 2005, p. 7.

67. Quoted in Amy Shipley, "Chemists Stay a Step Ahead of Drug Testers," *Washington Post*, October 18, 2005, p. E1.

68. Jendrick, *Dunks, Doubles, Doping*, p. 162.

69. Jendrick, *Dunks, Doubles, Doping*, p. 163.

70. Quoted in Christa Case Bryant, "Gatekeeper for Clean Sports," *Christian Science Monitor*, August 4, 2008. features.csmonitor.com/backstory/2008/08/04/qdope4.

71. Quoted in Josh Peter and Charles Robinson, "Believe It or Not: Clean Team USA?" Yahoo! Sports, August 5, 2008. sports.yahoo.com/olympics/news?slug=ys-olympicdoping080508&prov=yhoo&type=lgns.

72. Quoted in Alice Park, "What's Driving Dara Torres," *TIME*, August 4, 2008, p. 47.

73. Quoted in Park, "What's Driving Dara Torres," p. 47.

74. Quoted in Park, "What's Driving Dara Torres," p. 47.

75. *New York Times*, "Mark McGwire's Pep Pills," August 27, 1998, p. A22.

76. John Holberman, "Mark McGwire's Little Helper: The Androstenedione Debate," Think Muscle. www.thinkmuscle.com/articles/hoberman/mcgwire.htm.
77. Paul H.B. Shin, "Lance Armstrong on Doping: 'I Would Probably Do It Again,'" ABCnews.com, January 26, 2015. abcnews.go.com/Sports/lance-armstrong-doping/story?id=28491316
78. Sanjay Gupta, "The Truth About Steroids and Sports," CBS News.com, February 3, 2008. www.cbsnews.com/stories/2008/02/03/sunday/main3783478.shtml.

Association Against Steroid Abuse (AASA)
521 N. Sam Houston Pkwy. E.
Suite 635
Houston, TX 77060
www.steroidabuse.com
AASA is an educational organization that provides information and statistics on the dangers and issues of anabolic steroid abuse. Its website includes information about steroid abuse, steroids and sports, the law, steroid myths, steroids and women, and different types of steroids.

National Institute on Drug Abuse (NIDA)
6001 Executive Blvd.
Room 5213 MSC 9561
Bethesda, MD 20892
(301) 443-1124
www.drugabuse.gov
NIDA supports and conducts research on drug abuse—including the yearly Monitoring the Future Survey—to improve drug abuse prevention, treatment, and policy efforts.

Substance Abuse and Mental Health Services Administration
5600 Fishers Lane
Rockville, MD 20857
(877) 726-4727
www.samhsa.gov
SAMHSA is a government program that offers information about addiction, including quitting. People who are addicted to steroids, amphetamines, or other drugs can find information on the organization's website. The toll-free helpline is confidential.

U.S. Anti-Doping Agency (USADA)

5555 Tech Center Drive
Suite 200
Colorado Springs, CO 80919
(866) 601-2632
www.usada.org
USADA is the national anti-doping organization for the U.S. Olympics, Paralympics, and Pan American Games. USADA is responsible for testing athletes involved in these games for banned substances. Its anti-doping program researches banned substances. USADA also offers an educational program to inform athletes, coaches, and trainers about policies, procedures, athletes' rights and responsibilities, and the dangers and consequences of using banned substances in sports.

World Anti-Doping Agency (WADA)

Stock Exchange Tower
800 Place Victoria
Suite 1700
PO Box 120
Montreal, Quebec H4Z 1B7
Canada
(514) 904-9232
www.wada-ama.org
WADA is an international independent organization created to promote, coordinate, and monitor the fight against doping in sports. It developed the World Anti-Doping Code, which sets anti-doping policies, procedures, and regulations for all its participating nations. The code also includes the list of prohibited substances, exemptions for therapeutic use, rules for testing athletes, and protections for athletes' privacy.

For Further Reading

Books

Canseco, Jose. *Juiced: Wild Times, Rampant 'Roids, Smash Hits, and How Baseball Got Big.* New York, NY: Regan, 2005.
The former major leaguer writes a tell-all book about steroid use in baseball and names other players he claims have used steroids.

Clark, Dan. *Gladiator: A True Story of 'Roids, Rage, and Redemption.* New York, NY: Scribner, 2009.
The American Gladiator Nitro tells his story about how he came to use steroids, what his life was like on steroids, and how he eventually quit using them.

Elfrink, Tim, and Gus Garcia-Roberts. *Blood Sport: A-Rod and the Quest to End Baseball's Steroid Era.* New York, NY: Dutton, 2014.
The definitive and dramatic story of the Alex Rodriguez and Biogenesis scandal, written by the reporters who broke and covered the story.

Latta, Sarah L. *Investigate Steroids and Performance Drugs.* Berkeley Heights, NJ: Enslow Publishers, Inc., 2015.
The history of performance-enhancing drugs and how they became widespread in sports is discussed in detail, along with the effects of the drugs. Learn why athletes would risk their careers to take drugs that can be easily detected with a simple test.

Scott, Celicia. *Doping: Human Growth Hormone, Steroids, and Other Performance-Enhancing Drugs.* Broomall, PA: Mason Crest, 2015.

Performance-enhancing drugs can have some benefits for athletes, but these come at a high cost. Players risk various negative health effects, both in the short term and in the long term.

Websites

Anabolic Steroids
www.healthychildren.org/English/ages-stages/teen/substance-abuse/Pages/Anabolic-Steroids.aspx

The American Academy of Pediatricians has a section of its website devoted to substance abuse, including information from practicing pediatricians on the medical data and physical consequences of steroid abuse.

Anabolic Steroids and Young Adults
www.hormone.org/questions-and-answers/2010/anabolic-steroids-and-young-adults

The Hormone Health Network has compiled a fact sheet for young adults. This includes resources on hormone and drug abuse.

NIDA for Teens
teens.drugabuse.gov/drug-facts/anabolic-steroids

The National Institute on Drug Abuse runs a website geared toward teens and young adults on the abuse of various drugs, including anabolic steroids. Visitors to the website can find statistical and medical information as well as videos and blog posts.

ProCon: Sports and Drugs

sportsanddrugs.procon.org

ProCon.org, a website that explores all sides of controversial topics, has a section devoted to the use of drugs in professional sports. Articles on the website discuss what the different types of performance-enhancing drugs do, offer statistics on athletes who have been caught using them, and give differing opinions on whether these drugs should be allowed in sports and, if so, under what conditions.

Steroid Nation

grg51.typepad.com/steroid_nation

An online journal that examines the use of anabolic steroids and other performance-enhancing drugs in sports, youth, and society, written by physician Gary Gaffney from the University of Iowa, College of Medicine.

National Hockey League (NHL), 60
National Institute on Drug Abuse (NIDA), 40, 76
Nelson, Adam, 21–22
New Jersey, high school drug testing in, 72–74
Nieboer, Dan, 47
Noë, Alva, 52
norethandrolone, 77

O

Olympic Analytical Laboratory, 77
Olympic Games
  first documented use of steroids in, 18
  includes Adderall in list of banned substances, 15
  includes steroids in list of banned substances, 59, 61
  penalties for performance-enhancing drug use in, 60, 81
  use of steroids in, 18–22, 26, 47, 60, 62, 72, 82–83

P

Palmeiro, Rafael, 6, 8
Phelps, Michael, 83
Pound, Richard
  on athletes claiming never to have tested positive, 74
  on 1976 Montreal Games, 19
  on rules, 57–58
Price, Melissa, 78
Project Believe (U.S. Anti-Doping Agency), 83–84

R

Ramirez, Manny, 25
Roberts, Dionne, 42
Rodriguez, Alex, 6–8, 48, 50, 71, 86, 88
'roid rage, 35
Romanowski, Bill, 72, 79, 82

S

San Diego Union-Tribune (newspaper), 22
Selig, Bud, 11
Sheffield, Gary, 79
side effects
  of amphetamine, 13
  of HGH, 20
  of high doses, 29
  overview, 31–33
  in women, 35–38
Sosa, Sammy, 6, 10
Spitzer, Giselher, 37–38
Sports Illustrated (magazine), 7, 24, 70

Tygart, Travis, 84

About the Author

Jordan Rizzieri is the '90s-loving, five-foot-ten founder of the online magazine *The RPD Society*. She was raised on Long Island, NY, to love Alice Hoffman and Billy Joel and attended college in Fredonia, NY. Now she spends her daylight hours in Arlington, VA, with a dog named Gizmo, working as a freelance editor and writer.